THE Ph.D. EXPERIENCE

A Woman's Point of View

Edited by

Sue Vartuli

PRAEGER

PRAEGER SPECIAL STUDIES • PRAEGER SCIENTIFIC

Library of Congress Cataloging in Publication Data

Main entry under title:

The Ph.D. experience.

Bibliography: p.
Includes index.
1. Women college students—Ohio. 2. Doctor of
philosophy degree. 3. Ohio State University—Students.
I. Vartuli, Sue.
LC1664.03P47   378'.24   81-17797
ISBN 0-03-060036-7   AACR2

Published in 1982 by Praeger Publishers
CBS Educational and Professional Publishing
a Division of CBS. Inc.
521 Fifth Avenue, New York, New York 10175 U.S.A.

Printed in the United States of America

To all women who are aware of their potential

and who are seeking to achieve it

ACKNOWLEDGMENTS

I wish to thank the many individuals who aided in the efforts to complete this book. Specifically, I appreciate the support and helpful suggestions of Joseph L. Wolff, Patrick Vartuli, Maude C. Vartuli, Janice Vartuli, and Shirle Husted. I also want to acknowledge the technical assistance of Becky Burns in typing the manuscript.

CONTENTS

INTRODUCTION

The idea for this book grew from the conversations of female doctoral students at many social gatherings. The fantasy of writing a book on the graduate experience became a reality when 11 of these women agreed to contribute chapters.

The process of writing the book has been valuable to the authors. It has revealed just how common are the experiences and feelings that women encounter in pursuing the doctorate. Most of us felt isolated and removed from the mainstream of academe throughout the graduate years. This book helps explain in part why this was so.

The camaraderie the 11 authors shared was unequaled. Men have been through wars together and find their comrades to be lifelong friends. Although the graduate experience for women is not war, the strains it produces in some cases rival those endured in sustained armed combat. The intense experiences, the common anxieties, doubts, and concerns strengthened the friendship of these 11 women beyond measure. As do soldiers, these women shared a common "baptism of fire," and permanent bonds of friendship were established as a result.

At times, in the academic realm, personal experiences are discounted because they are not considered representative or generalizable. In the jargon of educational research, they are said to lack "external validity." But this book is not a research book in the technical sense; rather, it is a highly personal account of 11 women's experiences. These experiences are presented so that others may have a better subjective understanding of the ritualistic process called the graduate experience.

The focus of this book is what happens when a woman pursues a doctoral degree. It describes the doctoral experiences of 11 women in professional education at Ohio State University. The book has 12 chapters, each of which describes a different facet of the female Ph.D. experience. The first chapter gives a brief overview of this experience, sets the stage for the book, and provides the reader with an integrated picture of the Ph.D. process.

After giving an overview of the total experience, the authors begin to explore the motives of why people enter graduate school. Unlike many of their male counterparts, woman not only enter Ph.D. programs late—often only after their identities have been established through extended periods of intimacy, or after their feelings of competency have been confirmed through success in a number of increasingly responsible positions—but when they do enter they decide to do so tentatively and cautiously. "The dream," which emerges later for women than for men, is a fragile one and is continuously questioned and weighed against other roles and commitments. Adding to the strain of managing various roles and coping with pressures for academic excellence are two fears that appear unique to women: Am I sufficiently intelligent? Are the changes in attitude and expectations that occur in the Ph.D. process congruent with other aspects of my being?

Once students begin the Ph.D. program they face the hurdles of the doctoral process. For most students, the comprehensive exams are a proving ground. It is a time in which she must prove to the university that she is intelligent enough for them to spend time and money assisting her in getting the highest degree offered in her field of study. Being forced into this proving ground can make one feel very alone and very vulnerable. Many will probably question the wisdom of getting the degree, wondering whether the mental anguish is worth it. "High Noon: Surviving the Comprehensive Exams" is designed, as the title indicates, to serve as a guide for surviving this period with sanity and feelings of self-worth intact.

Another basic hurdle of the doctoral process is the writing of a dissertation. The chapter entitled "Taking a Giant Step: Writing the Dissertation" provides the reader with some basic information about the process of writing a dissertation. Some personal anecdotes of the author and other students are included to help the reader vicariously experience the full range of emotions encountered during this process.

"Surviving in a Predominantly White Male Institution" gives readers insight into the "old boy network" and the complex "games" of the male world. This chapter is important for every female who works in a predominantly male institution.

Stress is something with which each graduate student must cope, as it affects health and daily habits. In "New Brains for Old Bodies," the topic of stress in connection with the graduate process is explored.

One way of coping with stress is to establish a support network. "The Diary of a Web Spinner" relates how one support network was started, and conveys the value of this sort of group to each of its members.

Women can provide support for one another, but every woman has to resolve her personal relationships with the men in her life. "In and Out the Relationships: A Serious Game for the Woman Doctoral Student" is an examination of some of the concerns a woman has with intimate relationships. It has been observed by professors and students alike that the incidence of divorce and other relationship disturbances before, during, and after doctoral programs is high. This phenomenon may simply be a result of a larger societal trend; however, at times it would appear that there are problems in this area that are unique to the female doctoral student. Several distinct relationship modes that female doctoral students pursue are examined in this chapter.

More and more women are moving into graduate school, pursuing the doctoral degree while coping with marriage and motherhood. This trend is profoundly changing the relationship of women to their families and alters the nature of the graduate program, yet there is little institutional recognition of this. The struggles of the woman who is mother, wife, and student is related in "The Impossible Dream: The Ph.D., Marriage, and Family."

More mature women are also returning to graduate school and obtaining advanced degrees. "Grandma! What Big Plans You've Got!" describes the experiences of one grandmother as she returns to school to pursue the doctorate.

The purpose of "The Job Hunt" is to identify those areas in the job-hunt process that individuals can control and to suggest ideas about how to present oneself during the job search. Helpful suggestions are presented about preparing supporting materials, letters of application, and so on. The emotional pressures of waiting for a response from prospective employers are described, as well as the pressures associated with the job interview itself.

The journey that begins with the initial decision to pursue a doctoral degree and ends with obtaining a job after receiving the diploma is long and stressful. The last chapter, "Is the Ph.D. Experience Worth It?," is presented in the form of a dialogue among the 11 authors as they reflect on their graduate experiences. The discussion was centered on the value of higher education and the personal and professional changes that occur within it.

The women who contributed chapters are all successful, dedicated women who have thought deeply about their experiences and are committed to sharing their insights. The writers range in age from 27 to 54. Because this book has a personal slant, a brief glimpse into the authors' lives may prove to be helpful to the reader.

The general editor of the book, Dr. Sue Vartuli, is developing and teaching courses for the early childhood education undergraduate and graduate program at the University of Missouri - Kansas City. Professor Vartuli helped develop the child care center at Ohio State University and was an administrator-teacher at the center for five years. This book was an idea fostered by Dr. Vartuli. She wrote the overview, "A Professional Socialization Process," to give readers an integrated picture of the total Ph.D. process.

Dr. Rosemary Bolig, who wrote "The Ambivalent Decision," has been an assistant professor in the department of family development and human relations at Ohio State University for eight years. Previously, Dr. Bolig was involved in educational and play programs for hospitalized children and their families. She was the director of the child life department at Johns Hopkins Hospital for two years and spent a year in England working for the Save the Children Fund at the Hospital for Sick Children.

"High Noon: Surviving the Comprehensive Exams" was written by Mary Ann McConnell as she was going through her general exams. She drew from her feelings and frustrations to write this chapter. Ms. McConnell is a lecturer in the department of education, Xavier University, in Cincinnati, Ohio. Mary Ann has been an elementary school teacher, remedial reading teacher, field consultant, and editor for an educational publisher. She plans on finishing her doctoral degree by December 1981.

Dr. Bernice Smith is an assistant professor of education at the Ohio State University - Marion campus. Professor Smith has been a prekindergarten teacher and director of a Head Start Program. Dr. Smith wrote "Taking a Giant Step: Writing the Dissertation." Writing the dissertation was indeed a giant step for Dr. Smith because at that time she was a full-time mother, student, and wife.

"Surviving in a Predominantly White Male Institution" was written by Dr. Phyllis Levy. Dr. Levy is an educational writer and consultant. She has held a variety of teaching positions including grades two through eight, and university level. Dr. Levy has used her classroom to collect data to analyze the teaching process and student learning.

The graduate experience causes so much stress that a chapter, "New Brains for Old Bodies," is devoted to this issue. Sharon Barnett has worked on a stress research project and brings valuable insight and knowledge to this topic. Sharon is currently teaching early childhood education courses at Memphis State University. Previous to graduate school, Sharon was the director of continuing education at California Lutheran College. She was a faculty/field supervisor in human services at Western Washington University following an administrative appointment in supplementary training/continuing education at California State University - Chico. Sharon Barnett has served in Head Start programs over the past 12 years as a teacher, consultant, and child development associate (CDA) college instructor.

The need for support when one goes through a stressful, intense experience like a Ph.D. program was made clear by Dr. Katherine Tracey in her chapter "The Diary of a Web Spinner." Dr. Tracey is developing and directing a comprehensive school volunteer program for the school system of Sarasota County, Florida. She has taught German, worked as a middle school curriculum coordinator, and advised undergraduate students at Ohio State University. In addition to her career, Dr. Tracey has been raising her daughter— a web spinner of the future.

Dr. Rosalind Williams gives the reader an overview of the types of intimate relationships female doctoral students may have during graduate school in the chapter "In and Out the Relationships: A Serious Game for the Woman Doctoral Student." Roz has interests in mainstreaming handicapped children as well as parent-child interactions. She has taught at the University of Cincinnati as well as Ohio State University.

The problematic option of entering graduate school as a wife and mother is depicted by Dr. Linda Levstik in "The Impossible Dream: The Ph.D., Marriage, and Family." Dr. Levstik is still balancing roles of wife, mother, and professional career woman. She was a consultant with the state department of education in Ohio. She is currently an assistant professor at the University of Kentucky.

Professor Mary Cay Wells shares a mature woman's viewpoint of the Ph.D. experience in "Grandma! What Big Plans You've Got!: The Older Woman's Ph.D. Experience." Dr. Wells is assistant professor of education at Otterbein College, Westerville, Ohio. She has been an elementary classroom teacher and staff developer, and currently does consulting in teacher selection. Dr. Wells helped develop an open school program at Amherst. Some of Dr. Wells's support during her graduate experiences came from her two daughters, one son, and four grandchildren.

As one finishes the Ph.D. experience and graduates, the job search becomes very important. Professor Marion McNairy describes the process of how to get a job in "The Job Hunt." Dr. McNairy is an assistant professor of early childhood education at Indiana University. Previously, Dr. McNairy developed the infant educational program at the University Lab Day Care Center, Ohio University. She was a consultant to the University Day Care Center, Ohio University, for three years. Professor McNairy is also the mother of three sons.

The process of planning, writing, and discussing the book was worthwhile to the contributing authors. Together we refined, clarified, shared, and brainstormed ideas—the experience was invigorating. It was decided during one of our sessions to include feelings and facts from general and personal perspectives. Scholarly affective writing with an emphasis on the personal perspective characterizes this volume. Since the authors are all women, the book takes on a specific purpose and describes an important dimension of a predominantly male field. It is hoped that the product will be useful to readers interested in the woman's doctoral experience.

1

A PROFESSIONAL SOCIALIZATION PROCESS

Sue A. Vartuli

Throughout the Ph. D. process, I noted that many graduate students have similar feelings and experiences to
share. Although these feelings and experiences never
fell into a formal pattern, there were certain themes
that were repetitive. This chapter highlights the most
prominent themes occurring during the doctoral program. They will be dealt with in more detail in subsequent chapters.

The Ph. D. process varies according to the individual pursuing
the degree. The graduate student's attitudes, amount of support,
learning styles, self-concept, values, experiences, age, and sex
all contribute to different feelings, expectations, and experiences.
Everyone pursuing the doctoral degree has to jump certain hurdles.
The expectations, feelings, outcomes, satisfactions, stresses, and
experiences one (particularly a woman) encounters will be described
in this chapter.

When an individual enters the program there are certain motivational factors causing her to choose to continue her education.
The Ph. D. process begins before one has been accepted into the
graduate program. During the initial year, taking courses and, in
most cases, working as a graduate assistant provide experiences
that reveal phenomena associated with higher education. Comprehensives, or qualifying exams, or generals and writing and defending the dissertation are the two major tasks of obtaining the doctorate. The format, process, and importance of these two tasks vary
from department to department, college to college, university to
university. After the research phase of the experience, getting and
starting a new job complete the cycle.

This chapter will provide an overview of the process of obtaining a Ph.D. degree. The information was gleaned from interviews with female graduate students and recent Ph.D. graduates. The women interviewed also filled out measures of personal satisfaction. These measures helped identify the most stressful and intensive periods in the educational experience. There are a variety of ways resourceful people can survive this process.

REASONS FOR RETURNING TO GRADUATE SCHOOL

There are external and internal factors that determine if a person goes back to graduate school. Some of the women interviewed were motivated to teach at the university level, where a doctorate is required. Women already involved in university teaching are usually required to have a Ph.D. for tenure. As one student related:

> Well, I think it was a combination of factors. . . .
> There was external pressure to begin the graduate
> program to retain my position as a faculty mem-
> ber. . . . I had been out of school about $2\frac{1}{2}$ or 3
> years and I was interested in starting back to school—
> more for my own stimulation or new knowledge, but
> I would say possibly the primary reason for return-
> ing to school was the external.

Although some women are encouraged by professors or professionals to continue their education, the ultimate decision is a personal one (see Chapter 2).

Some personal needs are fulfilled when one pursues a Ph.D. Job burnout, a need for change, transition in life, and the challenge of learning are a few of the motivational factors that give impetus to women to return to graduate school.

> I had been teaching for three years and decided that my
> brain was going to atrophy if I didn't go some place
> where I could use it. There wasn't any kind of mental
> stimulation, or at least not what I wanted in the class-
> room. I guess I had burned out for classroom teaching.
> I wanted to do something different, to use the brain
> again and give myself time to decide what was going to
> come next. So, I applied to graduate school.

All the women returning to graduate school who were interviewed for this chapter were highly successful, intelligent individuals. Most came from well-paying jobs that required responsible decision making. They had respect and status in their jobs and were now beginning a new career endeavor. Their experiences during the first year were certainly revealing to these new graduate students.

THE FIRST YEAR

The change from respected professional to student can be a difficult adjustment. The program's initial year is usually marked by high anticipation, anxiety, and satisfaction.

> When I first came to graduate school, I was really excited about getting into the academic field and meeting people who were well known in the area of education. I had gotten a teaching assistantship in order to get financial assistance. I had a lot of difficulty adjusting to the tremendous change in salary because my previous year's salary had been over $20,000 and the TA was less than $6,000 a year. . . . I also got very anxious over my TA appointment because my appointment was changed four times. . . . The last change came about 2-4 days before classes started. . . . It meant very minimal time to prepare and get things together. I found out right away that if you wanted to know anything, you didn't go to the professional staff— you went to other graduate students. I think I probably found that out the first two or three weeks that I was on campus. The first quarter went well, but I really questioned whether or not I was going to be able to handle graduate school. It had been eight years since I had been in school and I really hadn't kept up with recent research and that type of thing. The job that I was in required a lot of writing work and took a lot of my time. . . . I had a tremendous amount of reading to do to catch up.

Accompanying the student role are feelings of self-doubt, distress, and inferiority. One student revealed she was afraid they would "find out" she was not capable or intelligent enough to pursue the Ph. D. degree.

> In some ways, the first year was the best year. I was
> scared. I guess you kind of go into it with the feeling
> that somebody is going to figure out that you are not as
> smart as you are supposed to be and I kept waiting for
> them to figure that out. For the most part nobody
> seemed to question my intelligence.

Because higher education emphasizes a left-brain mode or analytical
rationale of thinking, many women functioning in a predominantly
right-brained or holistic, creative way have feelings of defensive-
ness and inferiority.

During the first year the student becomes committed to her
academic discipline. There is an abundance of knowledge, theory,
and skills for students to assimilate. So much new information is
bombarding the brain that full accommodation is impossible. Seminars and informal discussions are a must for students to process
all the knowledge they are exposed to during this first year.

Another role that the first-year student usually encounters is
that of a graduate teaching or research assistant. She becomes an
apprentice in the profession. Some of the assignments graduate
students receive produce anxiety, conflict, and confusion. Students
teaching their first college courses are unsure of expectations and
are anxious about their own teaching skills. Frequently, little or
no support is provided by professors; on the other hand, some
women coming into the Ph.D. program find themselves overly
qualified for the positions to which they have been appointed.

> A mature woman friend of mine is now a TA in a degree
> program. . . . The head teacher is just a 24-year-old
> new graduate student and is her supervisor. This friend
> of mine is conscious enough to know she would have to
> play a certain role there. She can't take over, which
> would be so very natural for her to do. . . . Being a
> student makes you dependent because of other people's
> constant evaluation or telling you what to do. In some
> degree, subservient.

This does not further the student's personal growth and usually results in conflict between the student and the immediate supervisor.
Most of the time the assistantship appointment is one of learning
the skills of the trade, with or without guidance.

Students report having three main sources of personal support
throughout the graduate experience: advisers, peers, and family.
Professors, advisers, and committee members are all sources of
academic support. A male adviser sometimes becomes a father

image or authority figure. There are very few female role models in advisory capacities. Communication between student and adviser is often problematic. Some professors find it especially difficult to relate to women graduate students (see Chapter 5). Other professors get caught up in their own personal problems, including ego needs, and are not able to give support to graduate students.

Because feedback and reflections from major advisers are so important, graduate students need to select a person with whom they can work. Committee members must also be chosen with care, so no personality clashes arise between committee participants. Graduate students learn quickly that interpersonal relations play a vital part in obtaining a Ph.D. degree.

Fellow graduate students seem to be the most prominent sources of support and information for students.

> Probably the thing that I think concerns me most is that the major support that I've received is from my peer group and not from my professors—except from my one committee member. She has been really super. When I need to see her and sit down and talk, I can talk to her on a personal and on a professional level. I realized that after I had my first class with her. That is why I chose her to be on my committee because I knew I would get that kind of support from her. The rest of the support that I've gotten has been from my peer group.

Although family and nonuniversity friends are also sources for outside support, they rarely seem to fully understand the Ph.D. process (see Chapter 7).

Adjustments for students appear to be the most staggering the first year. For many students there is a loss of status, dropping from the role of a responsible member of society to one of being involved with jobs that are not viewed by students and faculty as worthwhile. As one student relates,

> I was all over the place working with all kinds of different people. I didn't really have an identity so I felt a kind of loss of status—you know, who am I?

Many times the graduate student is referred to as a "gopher" (meaning those who "go for" things that others need). This term certainly is not one of high status or prestige.

People returning to graduate school open themselves to exciting ideas, stressful times, criticism, and personal evaluation.

The first year opens students' eyes to the realities of the academic realm. It's a time when competition exists for the professors' interest and attention.

> The feeling of competition came from within me. It was not placed on me by other students. There were two students about which I developed in my mind an envy or jealousy and that was not usual. I don't tend to compete. I usually tend to do my own thing. I think of the multichanges; health factors and finding out that I was in a program where I was told some things would be available that weren't; I was really feeling off balance, and then I began to look around at other people. I developed a jealousy about what one student was doing and about the capabilities of another that had nothing to do with either of those people. I really liked them. The jealousy was not between them and me. It was something I was feeling on the inside. I was also hearing regularly from my chairman comparative statements about those people with myself which lowered my self-concept.

Some students' lives are further complicated by moving into a new city. Adaptation by families and spouses requires additional adjustments for the student. The Ph.D. process is complicated, to say the least, but survival means that you progress to the second year and comprehensive exams.

SECOND YEAR

The second year holds few surprises. Students are realistically aware of the Ph.D. process, courses become more manageable, and students feel a little more secure in their role as graduate students.

> I think as I watch the new students come in this year . . . there is a tendency by the faculty to make those first-year students work hard because they are so naive and don't know what is going on. I think you run them down the first year. The second-year students are wiser. A student came up to me and said, "Well, I'm sure wise as to what has been going on with the department chairman. Either you play the game or you don't play the game. That is the choice you have."

The second year is an intense time for studying because it is usually during the second year that most students attempt their "generals," qualifying exams, or comprehensive exams. Students are still assimilating what others know, and the process offers little opportunity to expand creative energy. Because the general exams are a major hurdle for graduate students, there is a separate chapter devoted to the process (Chapter 3); a general overview of the process of taking the exam follows.

GENERAL EXAMS

The attitude a graduate student has about generals is usually a result of the type of support she is receiving at that time. Positive support and feedback from an adviser, committee member, or professor can help the student view the experience in perspective.

> My major advisor was very clear, very good at helping students through that project [generals]. He had me go to each person and negotiate an area of questioning and get that in writing so that I knew what general topic they were going to ask me about. He made the whole sequence quite clear to me. I really couldn't bring it off without that. I knew what to expect. I knew in general what they would ask me about.

When students do not receive feedback and/or support about their capabilities, the prospect of taking general exams can be a fearsome ordeal. Listening to the experiences of other graduate students is helpful because it prepares the student for anything, although peers usually do not provide the best support before generals. Horror stories and experiences are related from year to year, sometimes causing undue anxiety and stress.

> I was petrified. I would have upset stomachs a year or so before I took generals—or really almost from the beginning of entering the program. Somehow I think it is perpetuated that that was the big, huge, horrible event in your life. People would sit around and talk about how they would throw up or faint or things like that. . . . You have to become somewhat insensitized. When it came down to the time I was really starting to organize and study for it, I was anxious, but that anxiety was so much more under control.

Some students avoid being on campus the quarter they take their exams and rely on outside support from family and friends.

Everyone entering the graduate program has more than a little anxiety about taking generals, yet the attitude toward the process can be positive.

> Coming up to generals is just as horrible as everybody tells you it is going to be. . . . I went in to see the people on my committee and that was very pleasant. Each of them spent lots of time with me talking about what to expect. . . . They gave me ideas—some gave fairly specific ideas about what they would be interested in having me talk about. Yeah, I was very lucky.

Some students look upon the comprehensives as professional enrichment. Generals can be a challenge, a climax to course taking. During the actual writing process emotions are usually intense, affect is high, and the experience can be confirming and affirming to the student with a positive attitude.

> Taking them [generals] was exhausting but I felt that I was really on top of it. I had more than I could possibly write in four hours on each one of the days. I wrote an incredible amount in that four hours, really, to look at it afterwards and say, "Did I do that?" That kind of euphoria lasted through the orals. It was for me a very positive, good experience, and I carried it through the summer feeling very pleased with myself.

While some students select creative alternatives to generals and develop publishable materials, for others, generals are the most horrible process ever experienced. The stress, rejection prospect, isolation because of intense studying, and self-pressure can make students physically sick. Students philosophically opposed to the intense writing and external evaluation usually have a very unpleasant experience.

> It was one of the most horrible experiences in my whole life. The committee members who had deep troubles gave me no support and had no idea where I was coming from. I was really at the breaking point. . . . The pressure that I put myself under really had to do with being philosophically opposed to the process. It was a degeneration instead of creation for me.

Taking exams is also viewed by some graduate students as a formality, another hoop to go through. That is, if a student buys into the system, she must pay the price. The student who takes this nonchalant attitude is almost desensitized to the external evaluation and pressures.

The realities of the exam are that they are time-consuming, stressful, and exhausting. One woman described the process of writing as "I laid down my life." It is definitely a time when students have the strongest base of general knowledge and information about their discipline.

Usually the attitude one has about writing is continued into the oral exam. It can be a euphoric experience or anticlimactic, a formality. It can be extremely negative, a farce, growthful, or even exhilarating. Students who enter the experience with confidence have usually had the benefit of positive feedback from their major adviser or committee concerning their capabilities. It is a milestone for the degree process. Many students at this point, depending on the type of experience they had during written exams and orals, elect to drop out of the program.

Postgenerals blues hit those students who have viewed the experience as an intense time. They are drained of energy and feel like social misfits. A type of depression exists for some students, and they cannot seem to focus on the next stage of their program— the research proposal and dissertation.

> Well, I think that the experience of doing the exams,
> particularly afterwards, was a down, a real down for
> a while. I felt as though I had isolated myself so
> much socially in order to get through the generals
> that I almost couldn't break back out again. I even
> remember one time not too long after I had taken the
> exam, getting ready to go to a party and thinking I
> don't want to go there. I didn't want to go anyplace.
> I didn't want to talk to other people.

Because of the intensity projected on the exams, a few students isolate themselves socially and cope with stress by overeating. For the students who feel comprehensives were a positive, vivid experience, the transition to research is made more easily.

DISSERTATION

Students experiencing high productivity after generals are completely absorbed by the dissertation task. But the research proposal can be quite a stumbling block for other students. Some find it difficult to switch gears, to become self-motivated. These students also find it hard to put their thoughts into words.

The hardest for me probably was first the proposal.
That was dreadful. I had never even seen a proposal
before. My adviser was no help at all. He had been
extremely supportive and very friendly. He gave me
all kinds of good feedback up until the time I began my
dissertation. Then it was like all of a sudden this
wall went up and I didn't know where to be with him.

It is another point at which many students drop out of the program.
The research phase of the process is one by which the graduate student turns into a contributor to the field of study. Research
for the dissertation will make some (usually minor) contribution to
the discipline in which she is studying. As they are writing the
proposal, graduate students usually realize how unimportant their
topic is. Being a one-woman team, one soon decides to generate a
research question that will be manageable.

I'm doing it on a topic I'm not very interested in because it is the easiest way out. The project I'm on will
take care of the funding and the data collection. I decided to go with the quick short route that is funded for
me. That's OK, but not exciting.

Dreams of making a significant contribution to the field get postponed until the first university job.
The total process of developing the dissertation is both time-
consuming and absorbing. Students find themselves dependent on
others for help, especially in areas in which they feel less competent, such as statistics or computer programming.

It is basically the fact that I do not have the statistical
background necessary for what I am doing. That is
not necessarily blaming anybody, for my committee
doesn't have the background. It is just that I have to
be at someone else's timing—specifically a statistician.
I can't always see someone when I have a question.

This dependency on others can be frustrating, especially when one
is trying to meet deadlines.
Overall, the task of writing a dissertation is utterly dependent
upon internal motivation (see Chapter 4). Students seem to feel
more in control of their lives and feel very little external pressure.
The process is not easy. As a matter of fact, some students report it is "the hardest thing I've ever done." One becomes egocentric and loses perspective on life. One almost goes through a

personality change. Simple delays become frustrating and alternatives to problems cannot be generated. The focus becomes narrow, so narrow that women lose a sense of the world around them.

It can be a very lonely experience. Many students find themselves isolated because they are consumed by the process. A key to understanding feelings about the dissertation experience lies in the amount and type of support a student obtains during the process. Advisers and committee members can give encouragement and information to help the process flow smoothly. The selection of committee members is a critical decision because advisers and committee members can also be major deterrents to the process.

As with the dissertation-writing process, the oral defense of the dissertation can be a rewarding or defeating experience depending on the feedback students receive concerning their work. If graduate students lack feedback, they tend to feel more nervous, insecure, and defensive.

> I didn't like the oral defense of my dissertation. I
> really didn't. I had worked myself up into a real snit
> about that because I hadn't gotten enough feedback
> from my adviser about the dissertation. He wrote
> me a one-page letter saying that it ranged from in-
> spired to pedantic. I was sure that most of it was
> pedantic and very little of it was inspired.

After investing so much time and energy in a project, students find that the dissertation becomes an extension of themselves. Some see the oral defense as defending who they are.

> When in generals I was just defending ideas . . . all
> the ideas in the dissertation were mine: from what
> was included, how it was done, to the arrangement of
> the research design. I felt very personally threat-
> ened by any kind of criticism of any of that. I think
> if I went into it again now, I wouldn't feel that way
> about it. I've distanced myself enough from it that
> now I don't take the criticism personally.

Personal pressures also hinder feelings of self-worth at this stage. If the student feels her own expectations are not met, then the process holds less satisfaction.

Graduate students receiving positive feedback on their dissertations tend to go into the oral defense confident and secure. The experience can actually be "fun." She is the expert, and a discussion of her work with colleagues is quite an ego boost.

GRADUATION

The ritual of graduation is valuable in that it puts closure on the Ph.D. experience. Graduation is a time of positive feelings, and the sense of accomplishment is high. Students feel graduation is ecstasy; poetry and sanity return. Graduation is a joyous time shared by family and friends.

Some students feel a lack of ambition right after graduation. They do not want to write or get involved with anything. For those students continuing in university teaching, publishing is a must. Perhaps it's knowing the pressures will start again as one pursues tenure that a breather is needed. After graduation is a good time to relax and regroup forces.

A JOB

While graduate students are involved in the process of the dissertation, they usually are looking for jobs at the same time. Since this is not an easy task it can be a hectic and stressful time. Job hunting is time-consuming, and most students view job selection as a major decision in their lives (see Chapters 9 and 11). Women with families and/or husbands find the process of job selection more complicated. The fewer factors one must balance on the job search, the better the likelihood of finding the right position in a highly competitive field. Some graduate students are not prepared for the rejection possibilities that accompany job hunting. Egos become involved and rejection can be the "pits." Remember that most students entering graduate school have not had experience at being unsuccessful. Graduation can be a disappointment if a student does not have a job. Postdoctoral employment at the university can amount to extended assistantship status. Some students feel a real loss of status when put into this particular situation. Most universities today prepare doctoral students for a limited number of careers—that is, teaching or research.

> As for getting a job, I'm trying to see . . . things with a broader perspective. This is one area where I don't think any major university prepares Ph.D.s to do anything but going to another university for a job. They do not tell you that there is a whole other world out there and that you are qualified for it. My adviser is not helpful about this at all. He graduated from big-name universities himself. . . . His idea of a job is to go to a major university, a tenure track position, become

brilliant, go to conventions, and write a lot in professional journals. This is a very traditional way of
looking at things and unfortunately hard to achieve
right now.

The limited preparation affects career choice and reduces potential
for jobs in the community, state, or federal government.

If the job-selecting process is the "pits," then being offered
a position is a definite "high," especially if you want the job. Beginning a new job may cause some anxiety and hassles, but the dependency and vulnerability associated with graduate school is over.
It can be a time of high creativity or a time of treading water if you
have to settle for a fill-in job until the family can move. Getting a
job is the icing on the cake. This is a time when students reflect:
"Well, perhaps it was worth it."

SOCIALIZATION PROCESS

In order to summarize the total Ph.D. experience, it is important to review the intense socialization process graduate students
go through. Students entering graduate school must realize that
they are entering a highly complex fraternity. The system has been
established and there are certain dues that must be paid. A woman
going through such an intense experience usually withdraws within
herself and becomes more egocentric. The egocentric characteristics of a preschooler return to be part of the graduate student's
psyche. Involvement in the real world is curtailed, and only immediate confrontations get attention. The gulf between studies and
the realities of life grows as the graduate student progresses through
the program. Probably the most narrowing experience is the dissertation. The focus becomes so intense and time-consuming that
students frequently lose almost all perspective on their lives.
Values are changed because the intense inward focus sets a pattern
of future interactions. Some people never resume the initial socialization level with which they entered the program.

The adolescent goes through identity stages that have been
associated with students pursuing their Ph.D.s. During adolescence
the youth tries on new roles much like a graduate student does.
The graduate student attempts to become a professor and researcher.
The professional identity is formed from reflections or feedback
from professors, peers, and self-evaluation. The dependency of
graduate students on feedback and evaluation from others leaves
them in a vulnerable place. Anxiety and self-doubt are bred in this
type of situation.

The lack of money also causes considerable anxiety for graduate students. Again, like an adolescent, the graduate student has to depend on financial assistance from others, including the university, family, or personal savings. Assistantship monies are usually below poverty level, and therefore the financial status of a graduate student plummets. Doctoral candidates visualize career aspirations, but must perform certain tasks or experiences before they "grow up."

Authority and power over one's life are temporarily lost while one is in graduate school. Students find themselves in subservient roles much like teenagers do. Lack of control over one's life is one of the hardest experiences with which graduate students must cope. Evaluation from course work, evaluation from an adviser, general exams, oral exams, feedback throughout the dissertation process, and defense of the dissertation leave students almost totally dependent upon external approbation.

The choice of adviser and committee is a decision that students must give much thought to because the impact of the feedback of these few people will have a profound effect on the student's self-image and consequently on the student's level of performance. As one graduate student summarized this process:

> We spend a whole year knocking down self-concept so
> that we spend the second year questioning who we are.
> By the third year we realize the self-concept has been
> knocked down and we are back to building it up and say-
> ing the heck with everybody else.

The socialization period through which the graduate student goes is intense. After obtaining the degree the graduate is ready to embark on a new career. The Ph.D. graduate has earned her rite of passage into the professional job world. The following chapters will examine specific aspects of the Ph.D. process in more detail.

BIBLIOGRAPHY

Heyns, Roger. "The Graduate Student: Teacher, Research Assistant or Scholar?" Graduate Journal, Vol. 7 (2), 1967.

Katz, Joseph, and Hartnett, Rodney, eds. Scholars in the Making: The Development of Graduate and Professional Students. Cambridge, Mass.: Ballinger, 1976.

2

THE AMBIVALENT DECISION

Rosemary A. Bolig

Why people choose certain careers has always been
intriguing to me. The motivating forces behind these
decisions are so varied. I explore the reasons why
woman choose to return to graduate school and obtain
a Ph.D. in this chapter.

The decision to pursue a doctorate is a major one for both men
and women. One may proceed directly from undergraduate through
master's to doctoral study, or return to doctoral study after professional experiences. There are various advantages and disadvantages
to both approaches. Continuing students may find the prospect of
prolongation of financial dependency (on family or institutions) a
major concern. Returning students often find the potential change
in roles, financial status, and (frequently) location significant factors in their deciding to return to academe. With increasing age,
and concurrently an increasing complexity of commitments and responsibilities to others, doctoral study often involves considerable
adjustment in life-style and stress for many individuals, as well as
for those close to the student (Barnett, 1982; Levstik, 1982;
Williams, 1982).

There are sex differences in the manner in which individuals
determine and achieve career goals and in related decision-making
processes (Super, 1957; VanDusen and Sheldon, 1978). Men who
pursue the doctorate appear not only to make necessary adjustments
in life-style more easily than do women, but they also are generally
more confident that pursuit of a doctorate is appropriate for them
and that they are capable of completing the degree. Having identified
career goals earlier in their development than most women, further

education is often an integral and planned part of men's career progression. Although there have been changes, men today are still expected to have one primary role (work), while women are expected to combine work and family roles. Women who choose nontraditional fields or identify careers in which direct progress to the doctorate is essential (for example, medicine), may exhibit career decision-making processes similar to men (Astin and Myient, 1971; Levine, 1969).

However, the majority of the women interviewed for this chapter, ranging in age from 27 to 54 and who are or were doctoral students in the field of education, indicated a different pattern in their ultimate pursuit of the doctorate. Most of these women began doctoral study in their early to mid-thirties after a series of successful and increasingly responsible professional experiences. Most stated that they cautiously entered doctoral study, often initially enrolling in only one course per quarter to determine academic competency or interest or ability to manage roles simultaneously. Throughout their studies most continued to analyze and question whether they could successfully complete the next phase of study (for example, course work, general examination, and dissertation), the meaning and purpose of their endeavors, and its cost to them both personally and professionally.

What led these women to make the decision to pursue a doctoral degree? How did they decide? What psychosocial dynamics were involved? Why did they appear so ambivalent? The answers to these questions are complex and sometimes as unique as the individuals themselves. Nevertheless, some commonalities emerged.

DECIDING TO DECIDE

Most of the women interviewed were children in the 1940s and 1950s when expectations and career choices for women were limited. Raised in nurturant families, from which they perceived support for their educational attainments and goals, they nevertheless had limited dreams:

> When I was quite young, my greatest dream was to be
> married and to have children. I was told what a wonder-
> ful "mommy" I'd be. It was, however, always expected
> by my parents that I'd go to college—to acquire a pro-
> fession or skills in case I'd need to support myself.
> Later I dreamed of becoming a physician—never a
> nurse—but discarded that because it would take too
> long and would interfere with marriage.

In retrospect I now see that my "dreams" of what I'd be were both limited and sex-role stereotyped: teacher and nurse. If anyone would have told me I'd go for a master's degree—let alone a Ph.D. —I would've thought them crazy.

Many of these women were cognizant as children that they were "bright." Some were early, spontaneous readers (for example, "In second grade I was reading on the twelfth-grade level"); many scored above the ninetieth percentile in achievement tests; others were aware that their IQs were high. By late junior high school, however, several of the women stated that their grades were no longer consistent with their potential. Adolescence for many presented a conflict between the motive to achieve and the motive to avoid success (Horner, 1969):

It wasn't as if I wanted to delimit my academic ability. It was just that I seemed to increasingly value social activities. I got, it seemed, more rewards from those activities, and thus spent less time on my studies.

I didn't really believe what the teen magazines were saying—that is, that girls shouldn't act too intelligent around men or be too competitive in sports. Yet, we often paired intelligence with unattractiveness. The "smart" girls weren't pretty. I think I adjusted my behavior to the middle ground.

The implicit and explicit message that many of these women received from teachers, counselors, peers, and family was that a career was acceptable if it was compatible with marriage and family. Thus most of the women interviewed chose traditional fields of study, predominantly education, upon entering college (Almquist, 1969; Tangri, 1970). The intent to have a job upon graduation and to combine this with marriage was one factor that may have differentiated these women from others in their cohort groups:

It was Autumn quarter of my senior year when I realized that my expectations of what I'd be doing after graduation were different from most of my friends. I was looking forward to obtaining a job and being on my own while they were panicked that they might not be engaged or married by June graduation!

Several of the women did marry soon after graduation but continued to work, primarily as teachers. By their mid-twenties most recognized that they were not just "working until . . .," but that they wanted to work and that their jobs were important to their self-esteem (Rand and Miller, 1972). Whether married or single this awareness frequently precipitated an examination of their abilities and knowledge and establishment of short-term career goals. Entry into a master's program was an outcome of this assessment for most. Acquisition of additional knowledge and skills directly applicable to their current positions was a primary motivation. A few indicated that the master's degree was a validation of their professional selves and provided the basis for the identification of the next step: pursuit of the doctorate. Some saw the master's degree as an opportunity to change careers.

During the process of the master's degree or soon thereafter, several women acquired academic mentors. (Two women mentioned that mentors had been found in undergraduate school; one continued this established relationship through five years of professional work and returned to the same institution to have this mentor become her formal adviser for master's degree study.) Not surprisingly, mentors were primarily male. The establishment of such a relationship may have been critical to the self-confidence of the women in learning what steps were involved in professional growth, and eventually to the decision to pursue a doctorate, as it has been for many men and women in nonacademic settings (Henning and Jardim, 1977).

A few of the women in their early twenties thought about eventually obtaining a doctorate. Some, through their positions in universities, became aware that a doctorate was essential to advance in their careers or to retain their positions. Yet the decision to pursue the doctorate was viewed as distinct from the previous one to pursue the master's:

> I just did the master's while I was teaching full-time.
> Pursuit of a Ph.D. was not part of my normal course
> of things. It was a complete break with my job and
> income, and a new life-style.

> The M.A. was a natural outgrowth of the position I was
> in at a university, and the process was integrated into
> my job. The M.A. was a necessity, but the Ph.D.
> was a "luxury" decision.

Although one of the women indicated that the pursuit of the doctorate was a "luxury," many of the others saw attainment of the doctorate as a necessity, especially if academic positions were the eventual goal. (Many indicated that they initially entered Ph.D. programs with this career expectation; others appeared to be socialized through the Ph.D. process into developing that goal.) However, in addition to the recognition of the relationship of obtaining a doctorate to a specific career goal, many of the women also stated that they decided to begin doctoral study for "self-satisfaction," "renewal," "stimulation," and "obtaining a warrant for professional identity." Few mentioned that initial reasons for entering doctoral study included opportunity to acquire skills essential for research, publication, and grant development that are critical to success in academic work.

This lack of early identification of the specifics required often led the women to perceive the nature of doctoral study, and to make decisions about courses and related experiences, differently than many men. Later in their programs, as they became increasingly aware of the skills that were valued, several women expressed frustration:

> Although I value all I've learned, I wish I had chosen
> an adviser who was actively involved in research.
> Then I might have begun to acquire the practical knowl-
> edge and skills I'll now need to do the dissertation, and
> in the future.

The "possibility" of obtaining a doctorate evolved through a series of successful professional and academic experiences and through the support and encouragement of others. Several of the women appeared to be forced into deciding rather than deciding for themselves; some were seeking change:

> I did the master's because I wanted to, but started the
> Ph.D. because I had to in order to retain my position.
> That didn't make it easier. I had to really think about
> whether I wanted the type of career—and life-style—
> that a Ph.D. seemed to be preparing me to assume.

> I was going through a divorce, and pursuing the doc-
> torate seemed like an exciting opportunity for change
> and self-renewal.

> It was the right time. It made sense at that point in
> my life and in my family's.

For others, the decision to pursue the doctorate appeared to symbolize taking control of their own professional, and frequently personal, destiny rather than attributing accomplishment to luck or chance (Frieze, 1975).

> I had been successful and rewarded in almost all I had undertaken. But many times I would feel "I was just lucky." I didn't really make any major decisions about my career. Things just happened. Then I decided that I would begin doctoral study.

> Making the decision to begin the Ph.D. meant putting myself first instead of my family. And it was a frightening decision. But I was ready.

The later entry into the pursuit of the terminal degree, often based on a later definition of career potential and career goals than for most men, appeared to be possible only when the women were ready to take "control" or to begin to address certain identity conflicts. First, the decision to begin doctoral study involved integration of professional and personal selves. No longer would "duality" of identity be able to be maintained (Henning and Jardim, 1977). The nature of doctoral study would demand almost total commitment of thought, time, energy, and financial resources for a period of at least three years. These demands would become more internally controllable upon obtaining a faculty position; nevertheless, the commitment required and expectations for productivity (for example, refereed publications, research grants) would be greater than in previous positions. Although all the women had begun this integration process prior to beginning doctoral study, the decision to do so presented additional uncertainties about potential change:

> I knew that I would change through the Ph.D. process, and although I wanted the Ph.D. and to change, I wasn't sure what that change would bring.

> I have changed . . . not yet in behaviors that others might be aware of, but in my attitude and expectations. I now value myself more, feel more confident, and am not afraid to put myself first.

The second conflict revolved around leaving traditional careers (for example, teaching) and becoming a "role innovator" (Tangri, 1970). Most of the women, though continuing in fields of education, felt that the doctorate would provide the opportunity and the obligation to create knowledge as well as to perpetuate it. Going beyond what they ever expected to do, hoping to obtain positions in academic settings still predominantly male, these women began to perceive themselves as pioneers (Nagely, 1971):

> I am aware that I am different from many professional women I know. I am more inquiring and more knowledgeable about theory and research.

> My friends who are in the public schools are content to go to work and come home to sit. Many hate their jobs. I am a doer. I like to help bring about change when it is needed.

Once having begun to resolve the aforementioned conflicts, the women applied to doctoral programs. Upon acceptance, however, several enrolled part time "to see if I could do it." Others enrolled full time, but questioned their capability:

> At times I felt as if someday "they" would find out that I was not really intellectually capable. For sure, I thought that would happen in the statistics and research courses. When I was successful with those courses, instead of thinking I'm okay, I thought, well there'll be another time when "they'll" find out.

> At the beginning I especially questioned my academic ability. As I had never done before, I compared myself to others. This didn't cause me to become more competitive, just less certain that I could make it.

Essential to the self-confidence of all the women interviewed (especially in the first few quarters), regardless of the support received from mentors, faculty, family, or nonacademic friends, was the establishment of relationships with other women doctoral students. These relationships were crucial for emotional support, sharing knowledge, and negotiating the "system":

> Even when I was enrolled part time I would find another female student as an "academic" friend. Before or after class we'd have coffee, share our feelings, analyze the course, discuss theories and research, and generally help one another.

> Through classes or by sharing an office we quickly identified one another. By the end of the first quarter we evolved a support group. Sometimes I had to

> make an effort to find time to be with these women,
> but without them I question whether I would've been
> able to complete the degree.

Thus women students often became models for one another (for example, "She's doing it—so can I"). The absence of adequate numbers of women faculty, and particularly women faculty at a point in their professional development capable of engaging in mentor roles, made the establishment of peer relationships essential not only for day-to-day survival, but also perhaps to completing the degree. For example, it has been found that women students with women advisers are more likely to complete study than women students with male advisers (Campbell, 1981).

SUMMARY

Despite the uncertainty and ambivalence most of the women expressed about beginning and continuing doctoral study, most have either completed or are near completion of the degree. The few others who are less advanced in their studies give every indication of completion. Several are employed in tenure-track academic positions; others, in high-level, educationally related but nonacademic positions; one remains a classroom teacher but is actively involved in writing and research.

Many of these women's career goals evolved through a series of successful professional and academic experiences rather than being self-determined early in their lives. They generally made the decision to pursue a doctorate through a developmental progression, rather than by a definitive decision to obtain a doctorate. Some began this decision-making process because they were self-motivated, often seeking to take control over their own lives, whereas others were initially externally motivated.

Dealing with a number of identity conflicts and a lack of knowledge of male-dominated systems, many began and proceeded through study with much trepidation. This ambivalence often appeared to be misinterpreted. As indicated earlier, the women frequently attributed their uncertainty to lack of ability. This belief was at times reinforced through overt or covert labeling by faculty of women Ph.D. students as "less committed," "less likely to complete," and "less likely to be productive" than male Ph.D. students. Simon, Clark, and Galway (1969), however, found in a study of women Ph.D.s (generally employed full time in academic positions) that differences in productivity (as measured by number of articles and number of books published as sole or senior author) between men and women and married and unmarried women were slight. Although this self-doubt continued throughout their studies, with each success it became less and less pervasive.

Ultimately, but at varying points, these women moved toward a feeling of "self-actualization" (Maslow, 1962). After the establishment of basic psychological safety, and a sense of competency and belonging, they were freed to become what they always had the potential to be:

I am no longer as concerned about what people think of "me." I know I'm okay.

Before falling asleep, I used to in my mind design research studies, build models, hypothesize relationships between variables.

There'll be new challenges, new adjustments ahead. But I don't think I'll ever question my ability in the way I've done heretofore.

SUGGESTIONS

It is essential that men and women become aware of the differential patterns of career development of the two sexes, and the psychosocial dynamics that contribute to differences (Mishler, 1975). Following this awareness, there may be less stereotyping; expectations for—and choices in—careers would be based on the individual, not according to sex, age, or marital status.

However, more opportunities and choices are available to women today than ever before, and it is assumed the career counseling for women is improving. The following suggestions are for women who now are considering pursuing a doctoral degree:

Recognize that the ambivalence and uncertainty you may feel is not unique to you nor necessarily a reflection of your intellectual ability or your ability to successfully complete doctoral study. Read about women's career development; talk with women doctoral students or women who have Ph.D.s.

Consider whether careers open to a doctorate in your field are consistent with your life goals. Analyze why you wish to enter doctoral study, what you expect to accomplish, and how you will prepare to meet those goals. Be specific.

Develop an informal program plan. Theoretical and research knowledge of the field and teaching skills are essential, but so are grant-writing, publication-writing, and research skills. In many institutions the publish-or-perish syndrome is a reality. Seek out a research assistantship rather than a teaching assistantship, especially if you have basic teaching competencies. Alternatively, arrange an independent study with a faculty member engaged in research to assist with proposal development, data collection, coding, and analysis. With faculty approval, write required papers for courses in a form that is publishable, with a specific journal in mind. Attempt to publish these papers.

If all other aspects are equal, choose a woman adviser or select a woman to be on your committee. Any woman who has been successful might serve as a model. However, those who have over-identified with the male system or those who want to be the only successful woman (that is, the "Queen Bee" syndrome) may be less supportive than many men.

Develop relationships with other women doctoral students (see Chapter 7). These relationships are essential for emotional support—particularly approval and acknowledgment—as well as for non-threatening sharing of knowledge.

Be somewhat circumspect in revealing your anxieties about your abilities and about "making it" to male students and faculty.

Observe male students and faculty. Determine what styles of interactions and behaviors they use that are successful in getting needs met, in getting recognition and informal rewards (see Chapter 5). Adaption of some of these strategies may be appropriate. Specifically, be alert that "exchange relationships" are frequently in operation between faculty and students. Take some control in striving for a balance between what you do and what you receive.

Be aware that change in your self-perception is inevitable. At times you will question your validity and at times your ability to persevere. Ultimately you will emerge from the doctoral process— with wings!

REFERENCES

Almquist, E. M. Occupational choice and career salience among college women. (Doctoral Dissertation, University of Kansas.) Ann Arbor, MI: University Microfilms, 1969. No. 69-21, 484.

Astin, H. S. , and Myient, T. Career development of young women during the post-high school years. Journal of Counseling Psychology, Monograph, 1971, 18, 369-393.

Barnett, S. New brains for old bodies: The impact of emotional and physical stress during the Ph.D. process. Chapter 6 of this volume.

Campbell, C. Women students and the need for female role models. Paper presented at the meeting of the Ohio Council of Family Relations, Columbus, Ohio, March 1981.

Frieze, I. H. Women's expectations for causal attributions of success and failure. In M. T. Shuck, S. S. Tangri, L. W. Hoffman (eds.) Women and Achievement: Social and Motivational Analysis. New York: Wiley, 1975, 158-169.

Hennig, M. , and Jardim, A. The Managerial Woman. New York: Pocket Books, 1977.

Horner, M. S. Fail: Bright women. Psychology Today, 1969, 3, 36-41.

Levine, A. G. Marital and occupational plans of women in professional schools: Law, medicine, nursing, teaching. (Doctoral Dissertation, Yale University.) Ann Arbor, MI: University Microfilms, 1969. No. 69-13, 353.

Levstik, L. The impossible dream: The Ph.D. , marriage, and family. Chapter 5 of this volume.

Maslow, A. Toward a Psychology of Being. New York: Van Nostrand, 1962.

Mishler, A. Barriers to the career development of women. In S. H. Osipow (ed.) Emerging Women: Career Analysis and Outlooks. Columbus, OH: Merrill, 1975, 117-146.

Nagely, D. L. Traditional and pioneer working mothers. Journal of Vocational Behavior, 1971, 1, 331-341.

Rand, L. M. , and Miller, A. L. A developmental cross-sectioning of women's career and marriage attitudes and life plans. Journal of Vocational Behavior, 1972, 2, 317-331.

Simon, R. J. , Clark, S. M. , and Galway, K. The woman Ph.D.: A recent profile. Social Problems, 1969, 15, 221-236.

Super, D. E. Career patterns and life stages. The Psychology of Careers. New York: Harper & Row, 1957.

Tangri, S. F. S. Role-innovation in occupational choice among college women. (Doctoral Dissertation, University of Michigan.) Ann Arbor, MI: University Microfilms, 1970. No. 70-4207.

Tyler, L. E. The antecedents of two varieties of vocational interests. Genetic Psychology Monographs, 1964, 70, 177-277.

VanDusen, R. A., and Sheldon, E. B. The changing status of American women: A life cycle perspective. In L. S. Hansen and R. S. Rapoze (eds.) Career Development and Counseling of Women. Springfield, IL: C. C. Thomas, 1978, 78-100.

Williams, R. In and out the relationships: A serious game for the woman doctoral student. Chapter 8 of this volume.

3

HIGH NOON: SURVIVING THE COMPREHENSIVE EXAMS

Mary Ann McConnell

While writing this chapter, I was in the process of
preparing for and taking my comprehensive exams
for doctoral candidacy at Ohio State University. This
chapter was written from the eye of the hurricane.

The image of Gary Cooper walking down the middle of a dusty
cowtown Main Street, head held high in the searing noonday sun,
moving toward a blazing, gun-shattering encounter with death is an
appropriate one for taking your comprehensive exams. At no time
during your struggle to attain a Ph.D., other than writing your dissertation, will you feel so alone.

For most doctoral students, the comprehensive exams are a
proving ground. It is a time in which you must prove to the university that you are intelligent enough for them to spend time and
money assisting you in getting the highest degree offered in your
field of study.

Being forced into this proving ground situation will make you
feel very alone and very vulnerable. You will probably question the
wisdom of getting the degree, wondering whether the mental anguish
is worth it. Do not stop. You can make it. The ideas in this chapter are the collected suggestions of a group of women graduate students who supported me and helped me survive the experience of
these exams. The chapter is designed, as the title indicates, to
help you survive this period with your sanity and feeling of self-
worth intact.

BEFORE THE EXAMS

Your first and possibly second year of graduate study will be devoted to course work. As you are taking courses, save all your notebooks, course syllabi, bibliographies, and papers. They are excellent reference materials for studying for the comprehensive exams and for helping you synthesize what you have learned.

The comprehensive exams serve to demonstrate not only what you know, but also your ability to synthesize ideas, design research, and realize the implications of those ideas and research in your field. It is important that you establish your own philosophy in regard to your areas of study. Once you have done this, your course work and reading can be used to develop facts and locate research that support your thinking.

Most graduate schools will recommend that you establish your committee as soon as possible. However, the only committee member that you need immediately is your major adviser, who will assist you in designing your program. Select your other committee members after you have taken courses with them and after you have found out what professors work well together. I decided on my committee members two quarters before taking the comprehensive exams.

In selecting committee members, you want people who are interested in helping you survive and grow through the experience, and not ones who are out to impress you and the other committee members with their scholastic brilliance. The committee members you choose do not have to be carried forward to your dissertation. If you are dissatisfied, you can change your committee for the dissertation. It is important to have at least one committee member to whom you can relate on both a professional and personal level. I found it helpful to have two female and two male committee members. My chairperson and major adviser was an over-fifty female renowned in my field. My second female member was approximately my age, well known in her field, and the member with whom I could relate both professionally and personally. My male committee members were younger and older also, and both respected my intellectual capabilities. All my committee members were most helpful in preparing me to take the comprehensive exams, but I had spent five quarters studying and deciding upon a committee in order to insure this type of assistance.

Once you have selected your committee, it is important to have at least one or two meetings with the group to find out what their expectations are and what they are willing to do to help you prepare for the exams. Keep in mind that your committee will usually not let you apply to take the comprehensive exams until they are sure you can pass them. It is personally embarrassing for you if you fail, but it is also embarrassing professionally for your committee members if you fail.

Establish what the purpose of taking comprehensive exams is at your institution and also check the alternatives for taking exams. Find out whether your committee is willing to write practice questions to help you prepare. Be sure you know the deadlines for applying for, taking, and completing the exams. Other graduate students can help you here, as well as your college office.

Graduate students are your best support group during this time because they know better than anyone else the turmoil you are experiencing. Pay attention to these students, especially those whose primary purpose is surviving graduate school with their sanity and feelings of self-worth intact. Their camaraderie and support will help you retain your objectivity and feeling of intellectual, emotional, and physical well-being (see Chapter 7).

Begin your physical, emotional, and intellectual preparation four to six weeks before you take the exams. Be sure you are physically fit. Four to five hours of writing over a three-to-five-day period is physically draining and requires preparation similar to that of an athlete. Take brisk walks, jog, swim, or do calisthenics. Some people find vigorous activity with their sexual partners adequate physical preparation. Pamper yourself emotionally. Congratulate yourself on being an intelligent, worthwhile person. Meditate, listen to music, read books totally unrelated to your exams, or spend time with close friends and relatives. You may find that getting a new hairdo or buying a new outfit (if you can afford it) is emotionally uplifting.

In preparing intellectually, identify constructs that represent your thinking on your topics. Look through notes, articles, and books to fit appropriate theories and research to these constructs. Remember that your committee members will be interested not only in your topical knowledge, but also in your ability to think creatively, to generalize, and to design research. Be prepared to cite names and dates, as well as facts, but remember that these must be balanced with your own thinking.

Find out what kinds of questions your committee members have written in the past. Examples of questions used in previous exams are usually available upon request from your college office. Discuss with your committee members what questions are appropriate to your areas of interest. Some committee members are willing to explain in a general way what they will be asking you in the comprehensive exam questions. Some members may be willing to write practice questions. After answering these questions, the committee members will read them and make suggestions for improving the quality of your answers. If I were to repeat this experience, I would ask for practice questions. Graduate students who have done so have revealed that they felt better prepared and more confident about taking the comprehensive exams. You might want to practice taking the test at least once, simulating the exam conditions exactly, or you may prefer to develop outlines for possible questions. Whatever you elect to do to prepare intellectually, remember to gain as much control over the situation as you possibly can.

Once you begin intensive preparation for the exams, set a schedule for studying. Spend four or five hours a day studying and then spend the rest of the time relaxing. Select the time of day when you work well. Different people work well at different times of the day. I spent the morning studying and then used the late afternoon and evening for relaxation. If you are working or teaching during the quarter you are taking exams, you will need to work out a schedule that allows you to fulfill your job requirements, prepare for the exams, and still have time for relaxation.

During the quarter you are taking exams, take no course work other than independent studies with your committee members. The requirement for completion of these independent studies can be that of writing your exams. This frees you to study for the exams only, and you are not faced with trying to complete requirements for course work other than your comprehensive exams. If circumstances force you to take course work during this quarter, inform the instructor that you are preparing for your comprehensive exams and discuss solutions to this problem (such as, completing assignments after you have taken the exams). I had to take two courses during my exam quarter and found that my instructors were most understanding and willing to be flexible.

Most graduate students are required to provide typewritten copies of their exams for their college and committee members. Find a cheap, accurate, and dependable typist, at least three to four weeks before the examination dates. Male graduate students often have wives or girlfriends who type their exams at no cost. Female graduate students have to pay unless they are lucky enough to have a spouse who types and is willing to do the work. Also locate the cheapest copying facilities that render good, readable copies. You will usually be required to provide a minimum of six copies of your exams. My expenses for taking exams amounted to $34 ($25 for the typist at 60¢ a page, and $9 for copying at 3¢ a page). Some students have paid as high as $60 or $70 for comprehensive exam expenses.

As the date for writing the comprehensive exams nears, you may find yourself dealing with stress-related problems (see Chapter 6). Friends revealed that they experienced nightmares, diarrhea, and stomachaches. Some experienced nausea and tension headaches. I suffered through tension headaches and a strong desire to flee the entire situation. The people closest to you must also be prepared for what will be happening to you. Perhaps reading this chapter or a similar document will provide them with a context for your experience. My sister, with whom I share an apartment, very patiently endured my tenseness, irritability, and absentmindedness because we had discussed what I would be going through.

Be prepared for the unexpected. It has happened that comprehensive exams have had to be postponed to another quarter because a committee member has had to be hospitalized, or has had to leave town because of a death or serious illness in the family. You may even experience one of these problems and need to postpone. Friends who have had to postpone the exams have stated that they felt more relaxed after the second scheduling, while others revealed that it added to the stress they felt.

DURING THE EXAMS

You will receive from your college office notification of the dates, times, and place of the comprehensive exams approximately one or two weeks before they are to be administered. You may wish to visit the area so you know where it is located and how long it will take you to get there to avoid being late. All candidates, in a given college, normally take their exams in one place. If this is not satisfactory, you may wish to check alternatives for writing your exams. Some universities allow graduate students to make arrangements to take their exams in a different location or at a different time. If you smoke, be sure to check what facilities are provided for smokers. Know where the restrooms and water fountains are located; if you must leave the examination room, you will not want to waste precious time trying to locate them. If you are an inveterate coffee or tea drinker, find out whether you are permitted to bring a thermos to the examination room. Because this time is exceedingly stressful, you will want to make any possible arrangements that add to your comfort.

Be sure to bring a watch as the examination room may not have a wall clock. Three or four hours may seem a long time for writing, but once you start the time flies by and you want to be sure that you have budgeted enough time to answer each question as fully as possible. Once you open the envelope of questions, determine how many questions you have to answer and how much time you can devote to each. Then stick to those time limits. I found it helpful to make a quick, rough outline for each question so I would not forget what I wanted to write. Other people have found it easier to start writing immediately and let the ideas flow.

Your committee members may allow you to specify on what day you wish to answer your questions. I chose to have what I considered my most difficult questions given the first day and my easiest questions on the last day. However, you must be prepared for the unexpected. You must be flexible. Be prepared to receive the wrong questions on the wrong day. You may have been promised choices. For example, one of my committee members said that he would probably write four or five questions and I would have the choice of answering two or three. I ended up with two questions, and answered both—and that happened on the first day, when I was the most tense.

Another problem that can occur is that of the ambiguous question—one written in such a manner that you are unable to determine what exactly is being requested. If this occurs, state, in your introductory paragraph, what you think is being requested, and proceed to answer the question as you have interpreted it. If necessary, point out the problem during the oral defense and ask the committee member if your interpretation was correct. If it was not, you can request clarification of the question and provide an answer at that time.

Some committee members find it helpful if, in your introductory paragraph, you explain how you will answer the question. This provides a structure to your answer and makes it easier to read.

You will need to check the particular procedures for handing in the exams and picking them up for typing and copying. If someone else is typing your exam, again, be prepared for the unexpected. The typist may omit a paragraph, misspell something, or may not have corrected errors you made while writing. This means additional time retyping. In proofreading, you may find that you neglected to answer part of a question. Do not panic if this occurs. Your oral defense provides time for you to elaborate on answers, as well as to fill in parts of questions you may have missed or did not have time to complete.

My typist was a friend who typed my general exams in the evenings after a full day at work. My answer to one question contained the same word in two sections of the same paragraph. In typing she had gone from the one word to the rest of the sentence following the second use of the word, which required retyping of the entire page. My writing was at times difficult to read, and she misread it. This is particularly true of unusual names of cited researchers. This required correction. We found it easiest for her to sit and correct as I proofread. I also found, during the proofreading, that I had neglected to answer part of a question.

The most traumatic experience I have heard was the student whose typist lost part of her written exam. Luckily, the student had made a copy of the exam before delivering it to the typist. If your typist is unknown to you, make a copy of the written exams before delivering them for typing—just in case.

Relax each day after you have finished writing. If you feel the need, spend only an hour or two reviewing for the next day's questions, and then spend the rest of the time relaxing. Read a good book, exercise, watch television, listen to music, or spend time with good friends. This allows you to rest better and to rise feeling refreshed and ready to go. It is also helpful to have someone meet you immediately following each day's exams so you can unwind. Women graduate students met me for lunch each day. They had all been through comprehensive exams themselves and were extremely supportive. Another friend, a graduate student who lived out of town, took time from her hectic schedule to call each evening to see how I was doing. Another graduate friend sent me humorous cards. Without this support group, I would have been a physical, emotional, and intellectual wreck by the time I had finished writing.

Your oral defense is normally scheduled five to ten days following the written exams. Be sure that the typewritten copies are turned in by the dates specified, and be sure that you have fulfilled all other obligations specified by the college. The day before your oral defense, reread your exams. Make notes about what you wish to add or expand upon so you feel confident and prepared when you meet with your committee and the graduate school representative. During the rest of the time between completing the written exams and the date of your oral defense, relax. My sister and her boss took me out to dinner at an expensive restaurant and then to a play. Another sister spent the weekend shopping and visiting with me. Several graduate students, who had also completed their exams or dissertations, gathered for a potluck swimming party at the home of a friend.

When you present yourself for your oral defense, present a calm and professional image. Dress in a businesslike manner. I survived classes and the written exams in blue jeans and cheap blouses, but for the oral defense I wore a much more professional outfit. Do not bring something for the committee to eat. This is a sex-role stereotype and inappropriate to the occasion (see Chapter 5).

Your chairperson conducts the meeting and will probably ask if you wish to add or expand upon anything you have written. Be prepared to do so immediately and confidently. The rest of the time will be spent answering the committee's questions. After the committee has finished, you may be asked to leave the room while they deliberate. The time you pace the halls may vary from five to fifteen or twenty minutes. You may find it helpful to have a friend who can pace with you. When you are called back into the room, learning that you have passed is a tremendously exhilarating experience. You will feel that you have made it as a scholar, and you may even feel prepared to go out and conquer the academic world.

If you have failed and your committee feels that it is necessary to repeat the comprehensive exams, you will feel absolutely defeated. Thank the committee for their time, explain that you will meet with them to determine what the next step should be for rescheduling, and leave immediately. Save your tears and anger for after you leave the room. I swore that if I failed, I would not repeat the experience. I could not see subjecting myself to the mental stress a second time. However, graduate students have failed, have taken the exams a second time, and have succeeded.

After a cooling-off period, schedule meetings with each committee member (in some cases, it may be only one committee member as you may have to rewrite only one set of questions) and discuss what steps need to be taken for repeating the exams. Additional course work may be recommended or further expansion may be suggested. Be sure that you know exactly what the committee members want; have them delineate specifically what caused the failure. Then, if you choose to repeat the experience, you will know exactly what is expected. One graduate student, who was required to rewrite only one set of questions, explained that she felt more relaxed in rewriting because she knew exactly what was needed to improve the original writing. Another graduate student explained that she was even more tense because she kept thinking about the ramifications of a second failure.

AFTER THE EXAMS

You have notified the college of the exam results, and in a state of euphoria you go home and celebrate. Prepare yourself and your family and friends for a nose dive. You will be physically, emotionally, and intellectually exhausted and may not feel like doing anything. This is the time for total relaxation. Do whatever you want to do. You deserve the time off. My recovery required two weeks. A friend stated that it was six months before she totally recovered from the comprehensive exam experience.

You may wish to spend time with people who matter to you. They will give your ego the strokes you really need at this time. You may feel like being alone and spending time getting reacquainted with yourself in an atmosphere untainted by academe. Whatever you elect to do following this experience, remember to pat yourself on the back. You made it!

4

TAKING THE GIANT STEP: WRITING THE DISSERTATION

Bernice D. Smith

One phase of the Ph.D. experience is that of writing
a dissertation. In this chapter, I have provided some
basic information about this process. Also included
are my personal experiences, as well as the experiences
of other students who are writing or who have written a
dissertation. I hope that in some way the reader can
vicariously experience the full range of emotions that I
felt during the entire process:

> Anxiety, when I first began the project
> Joy, that I had finally reached this stage
> Sadness, when things were not going well
> Happiness, each time I moved one step closer
>   to completing the project
> Fear, when self-doubt prevailed
> Love, when family and friends were supportive
> Ecstasy, when I finally made it!

INTRODUCTION

Writing a dissertation is the final step in the doctoral experience. Very often students look at this as if it were the all-encom-
passing experience; however, it is only a part of the process, not
the entire process. When one can enter this phase with this understanding, one can write and defend the dissertation with a wholesome
perspective.

At this point in one's educational career there should not be a question of whether or not the student should be in the Ph.D. program. Prior to this final phase, the student should have had many opportunities to write research papers and do scholarly presentations before her professors and fellow students. Many institutions provide these types of forums and seminars. Some schools encourage students to do presentations at conferences, and many institutions encourage students to begin writing articles for publication. When this is done, writing a dissertation becomes a natural extension of previous work and interest.

Although this may seem to be the logical approach, this does not apply to all students. Following the general examination, one student stated that she had no idea of what she wanted to pursue for her research project. One would assume that much of her course work would have related to a particular area of interest. Even if this were the case, this student could not think of anything for a research project. It had been four years since she took the general examination, and she had not begun working on her dissertation. This may be an extreme case, but it is cited here to show that writing the dissertation is not always a natural extension of one's previous work and interest.

Erik Erikson (1963) provides a framework for looking at human development. Erikson's eight stages of development encompass all ages of human life, and he sees personality formation as an ongoing process from infancy to adulthood. One interesting aspect of Erikson's theory is his emphasis on culture and society, which he believes help shape the individual, as the individual also helps shape society and culture. His psychosocial theory of human development is based upon the "epigenetic principle," that is, each stage of development builds upon the previous stage or stages of development.

In a very real sense, one goes through stages during the doctoral experience, and it is somewhat like the epigenetic principle. Each stage, each encounter, each failure, each success, and each challenge should prepare the student for the next stage, and each stage should logically build on the previous stage or stages.

THE INTERIM

When a student has completed the course work for the Ph.D. program and she and her adviser feel she is ready, she then takes the general examination (see Chapter 3). The examination, prepared and administered by the student's graduate committee, is designed to assess the student's knowledge of her chosen field. When the student has successfully completed the general examination and has met all other residence and credit-hour requirements, she is officially certified by the departmental graduate committee and admitted to candidacy to the graduate school.

Following the general examination, many students take some time to think about taking the next step. Although it may seem strange that a student would, at this point, ask "Why am I here?," "Will I be a statistic or a success?," and "Where do I go from here?," for many students this is a reality and may become a stumbling block that they can never overcome. Some students find that they can never take that giant step of writing the dissertation, and some begin, but never complete, the project. It is at this point that the often-heard statement, "I will never consider getting a Ph.D. because I will never be able to do a dissertation," seems to make sense. This is often a trying period because, in their moments of reflection, students often wonder if they will succeed or fail. Sometimes it helps to hear one's adviser or another professor say, "If we did not think you could make it, we would not have allowed you to go this far." Even the aftermath of reliving the general examination takes its toll. Those who complete the general examination with a good feeling may not waste time wondering about success or failure, but for those who literally had to "fight for their lives" during generals, then short interim periods may become very long ones. Some students can move right into working on the dissertation; others, however, may need a longer period of time before they can take this giant step. Whatever the case, those students who choose to move on may wonder if the dissertation-writing stage will be extremely difficult or if it will be a pleasurable and worthwhile experience.

STAGE ONE: THE BEGINNING

One of the most important steps in writing a dissertation is that of selecting a topic and defining the problem. How does one go about locating researchable problems? According to Warmbrod (1978) one can locate researchable problems from one's curiosity about a topic or from a desire to do something in a more efficient way. Research problems usually begin in one's general area of interest. The problem is then narrowed down to a subcategory of the general area. It is very important that one's study relate to a significant problem. No matter how objective a researcher makes her study and records it for others, her choice of a question (or hypothesis) to guide her research must always be her own personal question. Again, this is one of the most important steps in the process because it determines whether or not the researcher can manage the problem. Very often the researcher will start out with a problem that is too general, and it is only after she redefines and really tries to pinpoint what she wants to know that the problem becomes manageable.

When the problem is defined, the researcher can begin writing the proposal. Krathwohl (1976) listed the following questions to be asked regarding the problem statement:

Does the problem statement convince the reader of the importance of the proposal?
Is the problem one that has generality beyond the local scene?

Some characteristics of a properly stated problem are:

State in simplest form—a question is preferable.
Identify the variable being investigated.
Indicate the relationships between variables being investigated.
Identify the target population.

A well-developed proposal is basically a plan or blueprint for the research. Generally, it will have the following four divisions, which will become the structure of the dissertation itself:

The Proposal Title. This must clearly indicate key variables in the study, types of relationships between the variables and the target population to which the results may be applied.

Statement of the Problem. This section should give enough background so that the reader can see that this is really a problem. Arguments for the significance of the problem can be made, and the following questions may be addressed:

What new knowledge or product will be yielded by this piece of research?
Who can use this new knowledge or research?
How can this new knowledge or research be used to improve the state of affairs (Warmbrod, 1978)?

Related Research. The researcher should summarize the pertinent research and relate this to the proposed study. A theoretical base for the study should be established, and the researcher should show how this research differs from previous research.

Procedures and Methodology. Describing the procedural steps in details brings the project down to earth in operational terms (Krathwohl, 1976). This section should include population and sample, design, instrumentation and data collection, and analysis of data.

After the proposal has been written, the researcher presents it to her committee. Often a proposal that seems clear to the researcher may seem vague to the reader. Thus it may be valuable to have several others read the proposal before this presentation. If it is not clearly written, it will be returned to the researcher for revisions.

STAGE TWO: THE HIATUS

The writing of the proposal can be a great challenge. A well-written proposal can help the researcher move as smoothly as possible with the dissertation. Sometimes this may mean writing and rewriting the proposal; it may mean putting the proposal away and getting away from it for a while; often it means doing a great deal of thinking about the intentions and role of the committee, and why it seems to change (in terms of its expectations) each time there is a meeting. The many changes, suggestions, and frustrations can cause one to think, "If I can just get beyond this proposal, perhaps things will be all right." The constant working with the committee, making changes, and building on its suggestions and comments can cause one to think that this phase of the program is not smooth sailing at all.

Because the student interacts with, consults with, and works with her committee on a regular basis, it is very important that a great deal of consideration be given to the selection of committee members. It is important that all members of the committee work well together. Each student will need the kind of committee that can demand of her the quality of work she is capable of producing. Each student will also need a committee that can be firm and supportive and give her the kind of encouragement often needed in this final stage of the doctoral experience.

STAGE THREE: ACCEPTANCE OF THE PROPOSAL—A STEP FORWARD

It may seem as if this stage will never come; however, after many changes and revisions, the proposal is finally accepted. The amount of time taken to make revisions and changes will vary for each student. Some proposals are so clearly written that they are accepted when first presented to the committee. Other proposals may require minor changes, while others may require extensive revisions.

Writing the first chapter of the dissertation can be exciting because it is essentially an extension of the proposal. This can give one the incentive needed to move on to researching the literature.

The literature search is very time-consuming because there is usually so much information. This search is more extensive than the one done for the proposal. A complete chapter in the dissertation is usually devoted to a review of the literature. Students should make use of all the library resources, including the Mechanized Information Center, which will do a literature search for a small fee, and the research consultant who can identify all the important sources of information. The library becomes the researcher's second home, and many students find it necessary to set up a makeshift library at home. As they are comparing notes, students often talk about getting claustrophobia from seeing so many books at home. Some students reported that reading a microfiche for a long time can cause nausea and dizziness. One student found that taking Dramamine ten minutes before beginning her work solved her problem.

STAGE FOUR: DEVELOPING THE INSTRUMENT

For some the stage of developing an instrument is not as complicated as for others because not all types of research require instruments. Some researchers will decide to use an existing instrument. For some it is not that simple, because the existing instruments do not measure what the researcher wants to measure. Before this can be determined, the researcher needs to review the literature on available instruments. When the researcher is unable to find a suitable instrument, she makes the decision to develop one. The instrument must be valid; it should measure what it purports to measure. It must also be reliable, that is, it must be consistent and over a period of time it must measure what it purports to measure. The instrument items must not be selected at the whims of the researcher. A review of the literature can help here, and one can also turn to experts in the field. After the items have been selected, the instrument must be pilot-tested with a sample of the intended population. It is at this point that items that are too easy, too hard, or ambiguous must be eliminated so that the final instrument can be constructed.

STAGE FIVE: CONDUCTING THE STUDY

Conducting the actual study can be exciting, as well as frustrating. It can be exciting if the researcher has organized the procedures for conducting the study and has enlisted the help of persons to assist in collecting the data. Even the most organized and well-planned study does not always go as planned, but good organization can help things move smoothly. It is very important that the researcher set deadlines for receiving data. There must be some contingency for retrieving data that are not received by that deadline. Some researchers may have a telephone committee to remind people to return data. Others may send out letters as reminders. Of course, much of this will depend on the type of research being conducted. When experimental research is done, the experimenter has more control over the situation. When descriptive-survey research is done, this is not the case.

It is not unusual to find oneself changing deadlines when the data collection is not proceeding as anticipated. Recording the data as they are collected helps tremendously during this time.

STAGE SIX: ANALYSIS OF THE DATA

Earlier in the process, the researcher will have decided on an appropriate program to analyze the data (if this step is necessary). Students can receive help in this area from research assistants hired by the university. When the appropriate program is determined, computer cards must be keypunched and then fed into the computer. The computer printouts may look like Greek to one who does not understand statistics, but to a statistician there is usually no problem. The researcher should not, at this point, think that all she needs to do is feed the cards once into the computer. Very often this particular process is done over and over again. One little error on the cards can throw the entire program off. Sometimes the printouts do not have the complete program. One student discovered, after several tries, that she had used the wrong program to analyze her data. Somewhere along the way, someone had suggested the wrong program and she had to go back to the drawing board to determine an appropriate program. If any phase of the process can be downright frustrating or confusing, it is this phase. One very simple error can cause one to lose a lot of time.

When the printouts have given the complete analysis, interpretation of the data becomes the next step. Other graduate students who major in statistics (as well as one's adviser or committee) can be very helpful. One major problem at this point becomes that of the researcher making more claims for the research than can be supported by the data. It is important to make inferences and generalizations, but unsupported generalizations and claims must be avoided.

STAGE SEVEN: THE SECOND HIATUS—
A PERSONAL REASSESSMENT

Even at this point, self-doubt may still prevail. Writing a
dissertation can take one through all kinds of changes. The very
confident student can find herself thinking she does not know anything. Some students have to convince themselves that they have
come too far to quit. One student who took a job during the time
she was writing her dissertation, put her dissertation away for over
a year even though she was at the point of analyzing her data. She
stated that the pressures from her new job and fear of failing pre-
vented her from even looking at the dissertation. She said she was
afraid of her committee because they had not been as supportive of
her as she felt they could have been. It was not until a year later
that this student convinced herself that she had come too far to quit,
and was finally able to start working again on her dissertation.

"How is the dissertation coming?" is a question most doctoral
students hear over and over again. The reactions from students
vary. For some students answering this question is no problem;
for others it is a hardship. Many students report that they hate to
see certain people coming because they know what the first question
will be. One student told her best friend that she had not called her
because she had not done anything on her dissertation and she knew
the friend would ask how it was going. Some students develop pat
answers or say what they think the other person wants to hear.

There comes a low point when one must get away from the
dissertation altogether. Very often students will do anything to
avoid looking at the dissertation. Several students reported "getting in the car, just driving with no destination in mind," "having
an obsession about cleaning house or washing dishes," or watching
television even when there was nothing worth watching. These
things are done because students are now at a standstill and might
seriously wonder if they will ever complete this project if they do
not keep themselves occupied with other things.

What seems to help students at this point is the support of
family members, other students, and friends. No one, other than
those going through or those who have gone through the experience,
can fully understand what happens when a person sinks this low. It
means asking oneself over and over again, "Why am I doing this to
myself?" Only the most understanding of friends and family can
share these feelings and help one move beyond this point.

STAGE EIGHT: REVITALIZED, NEW ENERGY, NEW STRENGTH AND DETERMINATION— TAKING THE GIANT STEP

Those who endure cannot explain what happens, but somewhere along the way one receives new energy, new strength, new confidence and determination. Students will set new deadlines and will meet them. Students will work around the clock to complete a rough draft for the committee. The completed dissertation, bearing the written approval of all the members of the reading committee, is then presented to the graduate school office. The amazing thing about this stage is that the energy and will to succeed are there, and the student performs with renewed interest.

STAGE NINE: GLORY OR AGONY

Hearing the committee's acceptance of the dissertation is like rejoicing at the birth of a child. It makes all the hard work and suffering seem worthwhile. It is as if a burden has been lifted from one's shoulders.

The next step is defending the dissertation. This experience is different for each student. Much will depend on the quality of research done, the kind of rapport one has with the committee, and the amount of ego strength that one has at the end of this whole process. For some students it is agony. The committee may be rough and the student may be very anxious. These students go in thinking that the committee will try to trick them. In essence, they have set the tone for their own defense.

Other students may experience complete ecstasy because they feel that writing the dissertation is one of the most creative things they have ever done. These students usually feel good about what they have done, and they go in with the attitude that they know more about their dissertation than anyone else does. They enter with a willingness to share this knowledge.

Reactions to the defense are as varied as the defense itself. Some students end up with ambivalent feelings; others are so relieved to have finished that they do not know exactly how they feel. Many students are simply happy because the defense has gone very well for them. Although the feelings may be different, no one will deny that a real sense of accomplishment is there. No one can destroy that.

STAGE TEN: THE FINALE

There are many last-minute details that must be taken care of following the defense of the dissertation. Corrections must be made. Typed copies must be given to the adviser and to the graduate school (many students also give copies to their committee members). The complete cost of the dissertation, having the dissertation typed and copies made, and paying the graduation fees make students realize that completing the dissertation can be a financial drain. Even at this point some students feel that someone will find something wrong at the last minute. Looking at the graduation list several times, making sure one's name is on the list, is a common occurrence among students. When all this is done and the student finally graduates, she can truly say, "I finally made it!"

REFERENCES

Erikson, Erik H. Childhood and Society. New York: Norton, 1963.

Krathwohl, David R. How to prepare a research proposal. Syracuse, N.Y.: Syracuse University Book Store, 1976.

Van Dalen, Deobold B. Understanding Educational Research. New York: McGraw-Hill, 1973.

Warmbrod. Selecting and defending a research problem. Lecture given at Ohio State University, Columbus, Ohio, January 11, 1978.

5

SURVIVING IN A PREDOMINANTLY WHITE MALE INSTITUTION

Phyllis Saltzman Levy

The information in this chapter has had a great impact on my ability to get done what I need to accomplish. It has increased my professional productivity and happiness because I have learned to avoid unnecessary grief. My intent in taking the time to write it down is to share this with other women. I hope each woman, based on her individual situation and intuition, will filter this information and alter usable portions to fit her needs.

I was sitting in his office. Having done a recent intensive study as part of my doctoral work, I was the expert on campus on the topic under discussion. He asked good questions. He had provided me with excellent resources to study. I felt that I was making headway with my professor, that I was being given respect because of my achievements.

We were interrupted. Since we both knew that our appointed time was limited, I assumed he would make it a brief chat. The male who stood in the doorway wanted a tennis date with my professor. It was accepted, but they needed two more players. They began checking with other male professors. Then they checked with the male doctoral candidates. They even asked the male student who had joined the discussion with me. They still needed a fourth.

During this fifteen-minute episode, I was not invited to join them, nor was my presence in the room even noted. From the status of the competent colleague, I had tumbled to the status of a chair. The

time scheduled for my appointment was over. Half
had been wasted. The task was not completed. And
it was clear to me that I was not part of the inner
circle.

In any bureaucracy, much of the important work is done during informal social time. Playing tennis is one example. Going to
lunch and going out for a Friday beer are other examples. Certainly, business can be accomplished without these social activities.
But to be arbitrarily excluded from them on the basis of sex hurts.
Inclusion in such activities would mean forming stronger links with
the white males who presently hold the power positions. This would
affect one's experience as a graduate student as well as one's future
on the job market. This chapter will take an in-depth look at the
role of women in a male-dominated field.

STUDENT STATUS

With few exceptions, there are advantages while male students
have that female students miss. This is a partial listing of such
"goodies":

- Being invited to assist professors in giving workshops;
- Going on trips out of state with professors to meet colleagues at
  other institutions;
- Getting paid consulting jobs through recommendations of pro-
  fessors;
- Getting desks in central locations;
- Getting offices as graduate students;
- Being encouraged to write grants for support;
- Getting articles, papers, and dissertations typed without per-
  sonal expense for the work;
- Getting the individualized tutoring and attention from male pro-
  fessors that occurs over lunch, drinks, tennis, or other informal
  social times. This includes time to experiment with ideas and
  getting feedback as they form; and
- Writing for publication with professors and having both names
  appear as coauthors.

This list was compiled from the real experiences, or lack of experiences, of the contributors to this book.

Female graduate students are treated differently by male professors. "You're doing this for both of us" and "Can you see that
this gets typed?" are two statements made to women by male pro-

fessors. Women are encouraged in the college of education to become teacher-educators; they are frequently discouraged from becoming researchers. Female students with families are rarely seen as needing financial support as much as male students with families. The difference in treatment and expectations of women causes the female student to wonder about her own status.

Obviously, there are reasons for female students being treated differently. Many adult males are simply uncomfortable with women. Men often do not know how to communicate with women as equals and competent professionals; they have experience only in playing the roles of son, brother, husband, father, and sex partner and cannot play the role of friend or colleague. Finally, there are those men who cannot see a woman as anything but an object for sex. The validity of these reasons is questionable.

In the school system as it now exists:

> Males are likely to receive support all along from parents and teachers [to achieve academically], while women are less likely to have parental encouragement from an early age, but may receive it once they consider graduate work during or after college. Women are more likely than men to receive support from contemporaries . . . and their mate. (From research summarized by Adler in Katz and Hartnett, 1976, p. 203)

Thus, in addition to different overt behaviors between treatment of male and female doctoral students, women have had to find untraditional support systems to achieve what they have as students.

A THEORETICAL BASE: DR. ANNE WILSON SCHAEF

Psychiatrist Anne Wilson Schaef (1978) has done some interesting research into the different ways white males and white females construe the world.* Shaef believes there are four major myths about white male society. First, white male society is the only one that exists. These men often say, "This is the way it

---

*Schaef characterizes minority world views as different from the white male view. This chapter was written by a white woman, and therefore cannot necessarily be generalized to women of other colors.

works" or "It can't be done that way." They use this as a statement
of truth. (The obvious and most effective response to such a statement is "Why?") Second, white male society is innately superior to
everything else. Third, this system knows all and understands all.
This belief is so strong that other forms of power are not even explored. Finally, white male society believes that it is possible to
be logical, rational, and objective at all times. This belief suits
predominantly left-brained, sequential thinkers. These myths are
the basis of much of what goes on at universities.

These myths have been applied to the academic world with regard to the female student:

> subtle forms of discrimination stem from the nature of
> the present academic world. The prescribed academic
> style is often unfamiliar and incongruent with women's
> styles. Norms governing academic life (e.g., which
> activities are valued and rewarded, which behaviors
> or attitudes are viewed as professional or nonprofes-
> sional) are male-based and are ethnocentric insofar
> as they are taken to be the only appropriate or cor-
> rect standards of merit. Thus, female as well as
> male students may be forced either to leave the insti-
> tution or [play the game]. (Adler in Katz and Hartnett,
> 1976, p. 207)

If the choice were only to leave or to play the game as it now exists,
many of us would not have completed our doctoral work. A third alternative is to learn how to play the game with regard to fairly super-
ficial behaviors in order to preserve the self while attending graduate school.

Schaef's research shows that women do not trust or like each
other very much. They compete for male validation (we female doctoral candidates are especially good at this). Women see females
as innately inferior to males. Women believe in fairness. They
also believe that the white male society will be fair; so they go
about trying to learn "the rules." Once they know the rules inside
out, women discover that the rules change for them and that white
males often do not abide by the rules. Then women say, "This
isn't fair." Moreover, Schaef says women have an externally developed identity, including a void. This void is filled by a male;
the woman finds identity in being the husband's wife or the child's
mother. Often it is difficult to understand these characteristics or
to comprehend how deeply these beliefs are held by women.

Schaef compares the white male system to a religion. Its
basic tenet is the scientific method. However, there are problems

when the scientific method takes on religious overtones. There is a belief in the reality of numbers: "You can measure anything; if you can measure, you can predict; if you can predict, you can control," and control is what power is all about. This belief is the basis for much of research, that area from which the participant gleans status and success in the university community. The white male society has no theology of differences. Differences are seen as a threat. By definition, this is a racist, sexist "religion."

Schaef establishes dichotomies of several concepts. She compares the understandings of white male society to female society. The concepts include responsibility, intimacy, relationships, the center of one's universe, and dualism versus multivariance.

The first concept is responsibility. White males construe responsibility as accountability. They want to know who is to blame when something goes wrong. Females construe responsibility to mean the ability to respond. They want to know who does what when a solution is needed to a problem.

The second concept is intimacy. White males see intimacy as physical; females see it as verbal. Schaef tells the story of a couple who came to her to discuss their sexual problems (note the physical basis of the definition of the problem: the problem is defined in the male mode). He would travel often. On his way home, he would think about the sex he and his wife would experience upon his arrival. As he traveled home, she thought about all the things she wanted to tell him, to share with him. There was always a clash of agenda when he arrived. Schaef redefined the problem as an intimacy problem and proceeded to help them solve it.

The third concept is that of relationships. White males behave in a "one-up, one-down" manner in a relationship. Women behave in a peer manner unless forced to behave otherwise. This behavior pattern is stronger for women than the need to be equal. Thus, when confronted with one-up, one-down experiences, women often continue to play peer.

The fourth concept has to do with the perceived center of the universe. Generally, white males see themselves and their work as the center. Women see relationships as the center (see Chapter 8). Every aspect of one's life has to go through, be defined by, and be related to either profession-centeredness or relation-centeredness. Each of these foci dictates priorities for the individual.

The fifth concept is dualism-multivariance. Generally, white males see the world as dualistic. For example, if one says the female system is real and valuable, this would imply for them that the male system is not. The female system is multivariant. Women can say, "I'm right, but this doesn't mean you're wrong, we both can be right." Schaef says that dualistic thinking is a form of mind con-

trol being taught in public schools. It limits thinking to 10 percent
of the brain's capacity. The brain has the capacity to raise the
complexity level of understanding from dualism to multivariance.
Each of these five explanations of concepts helps one to understand
better why communication at a white male-controlled institution,
such as a university, is difficult for women.

My reaction to Schaef's comments was one of relief. The
message I heard was that the way I construed my world, even though
it was obviously different from the power structure, was all right.
She helped me to understand the way I was being viewed by those
who owned the power. Schaef gave me power to successfully oper-
ate in this system. She taught me the way the "opposition" thought.
This freed me to behave knowledgeably. For example, I began to
understand the appropriate times for me to play one-up, one-down,
even though this was not my natural style. She also taught me what
my male professors meant when they asked who was going to be responsible. With such information, I could easily maintain my own
integrity and still succeed at playing the university game.

Research done by others has shown that women often fear success (Horner cited in Gilligan, 1979, p. 438). The implications of
this are frightening when considered in regard to the famale doctoral student. The student may "buy into" the white male system,
taking an always inferior stance. If this is the case, reevaluation
of personal goals might be appropriate.

Gilligan (1979) develops the notion that women have a "concep-
tion of self and morality" (p. 445) different from the male concep-
tion. This certainly has an impact on a woman's success in the
academic world.

Change is possible. The differences in behavior patterns can
have an impact on the dominant university culture. Adler (in Katz
and Hartnett, 1976) proposes that the increase in the number of
women in professional capacities may cause changes in the "structure of inquiry":

> Women often prefer cooperative to competitive modes
> and may be more likely than men to engage in coopera-
> tive research. . . . [And since men too are beginning to
> realize the disadvantages of competition,] professional
> behavior may shift from competition and empire-
> building to cooperative joint ventures. (p. 220)

This possibility would increase the opportunities for both creative
women and men to make contributions to their fields. However,
Adler (p. 221) does note that the likelihood of such a change is not
great, due to existing pressures such as economic cuts.

THE UNIVERSITY GAME

For the female doctoral student, learning to play the university game often must be self-taught. She rarely is tutored by one who understands it. The game includes:

- How to prepare for, have an influence on the creation of, and take qualifying examinations (see Chapter 3);
- How to write papers;
- How to publish;
- What conferences one should attend;
- How to apply to present papers at conferences;
- How to address conferences;
- How to work with a male adviser;
- How to work with her committee;
- How to work with male and female graduate students;
- Which courses to choose;
- How to teach adult males when a teaching associate;
- How to be taken seriously at meetings;
- How to press for an answer;
- How to get money for support, including writing grants; and
- What needs to be done as a graduate student to increase the probability of success on the job market (see Chapter 11).

Many of these will be elaborated upon in other chapters of this book. I will restrict my comments to telling a few stories appropriate to my survival as a woman in a white male institution.

Writing papers for classes is a major part of graduate school work. I learned how to write professional quality papers in a very painful way. I had done what I thought was an outstanding job on a paper. I had included resources in three languages as well as extensive visual examples of the concept. I was very proud to turn in this paper to my white male professor. I had been working with him for several quarters and finally felt I had succeeded in producing a "scholarly" document. The paper was returned to me with this written on the title page:

> B-
> The material is interesting and the paper is well written. The shortcoming is that you have said only the most obvious things about the art work which you have examined. I do not feel that you have worked closely with the material and scrutinized it carefully.

It hurt. The criticism was clear. How to improve my analysis was not. The tutoring I needed occurred for others in this professor's office. Nonverbal messages, however, indicated to me that I was not welcome to participate in this activity. Because of this void, I enlisted the help of my husband, who is an attorney and is excellent at playing the white male game. My husband has since become my tutor and adviser on how to play it. We sat down and, in a few hours, he taught me how to write. He showed me where elaboration was needed by the sequential, logical thinker. He introduced questions such as "Why?," "So what?," "What does this mean?," "How are these related?," which I have since used in all my writing. Previously, my writing consisted of making intuitive generalizations based on the data. I had assumed that these were clear. The messages my husband gave me were that they were not and that they were worthy of clarification. I was lucky to have a tutor who was willing to help me learn how to play the game. He taught me to write about the connections and relationships in a scientific, white male, and professional way.

A black female doctoral student made this comment: "Many professors believe that blacks in general cannot write; consequently, many black students realize that certain professors will never give an A to a black student, even though she or he may deserve it."

She substantiated this statement with several examples:

> A black student turned in a research paper to a professor, and in returning the paper to the student, the professor commented, "I did not know blacks could write like that."
>
> One student who made A's on all of her papers until this professor [who refused to give A's to blacks] discovered she was black [then], the grades changed to B's.
>
> A black female student was accused of not writing her dissertation. She had to prove to her adviser and committee that she had done the work. [This student had received only A's and positive feedback throughout her doctoral studies from the same professors.]

It is clear that the challenges for a black female student are greater than for a white female student when trying to survive the predominantly white male system.

My husband continued to tutor me when I wanted to learn how to publish. His main messages were do not be cheap and do not beg or try to convince. I began to have the typing done on quality paper by a professional secretary who used an IBM machine. I freed myself to make all the copies I needed. And I learned to write a concise, male-like cover-letter on expensive stationery printed with my own letterhead:

> Dear (name of editor):
> Enclosed please find a copy of ("name of article").
> Your consideration of it for publication in (name of journal) would be appreciated.

In the cover letter, I did not try to convince the editor that my article was worthy of consideration; I assumed this fact. I did not write about all my friends and colleagues who were impressed by it and were sure it should be published. I had to learn to get through the editor's door the way white males do.

I had another challenge when I began teaching adult white males at the university. Most of them were receptive, or at least did not express a need to "put me in my place." But there were one or two a quarter who felt the need to disrupt the continuity of the course by playing one-up, one-down with me. This was very difficult at first, but as I learned more and more about the white male game and what was behind it, the challenge became easier. I found that what I wore to class when teaching had a strong impact on the way I was received (Molloy, 1977). What was occurring here was not directed at the person, Phyllis Levy. It was simply part of the white male game. They were doing a general assessment of what I represented. My clothing and my femaleness were parts of this. I decided that if I were forced to play one-up, one-down, I was never going to finish in the down position. I learned that the most effective way to stop such a power confrontation from continuing was to encourage the class to respond to what the white male was stating as fact. For example, the male student would make a statement such as "That won't work in the public schools" in response to something I had presented in class. Rather than repeating my position, I now say to the class, "What do you think? Will it work?" This technique has never failed me. Success at classroom management when adult males are present as students is difficult for the female instructor but not unattainable.

In addition, others have examined the university game with regard to female students functioning within it. Hartnett (Katz and Hartnett, 1976) discusses the importance of "the extent to which students feel accepted and respected by members of the faculty, the degree to which the students are able to relate to members of the faculty as friends and colleagues" (p. 59). Adler (Katz and Hartnett, 1976) identifies such relationships with faculty members as extremely problematic for female students: "a female student is less likely than a male to be taken on as a protégé and may not form close relationships with faculty" (p. 209). When these statements are superimposed, it becomes clear that one of the most significant aspects of graduate student life is very difficult for women to experience. Adler noted the result:

> The female students in their [Wright Institute] sample reported significantly fewer discussions with faculty outside the office, fewer total discussions with their research advisor, and fewer discussions with their advisor about the advisor's research interests than did male students. (p. 210)

Such results take their toll on the richness of the graduate experience.

BE CONSCIOUS OF THE MESSAGE YOU ARE SENDING

Below is a list of behaviors I consciously avoid. I believe that they could permanently damage my professional, equal status if done in the white male institution.

Avoid baking cookies for meetings. If the participants have agreed that each will take a turn in providing refreshments, I buy a box of doughnuts or a bag of potato chips. If I had a wife to do my baking for me, I might consider bringing cookies. I deliberately mimic the behaviors of the white males in power by contributing food to meetings as they do.

Avoid answering the communal phone. If you do, you will certainly be asked to take a message. The assumption is that you, because you are female, are the secretary.

Avoid cleaning up after meetings. It is not your job. If you do it, you are proving that you like it and would really prefer to be in the role of keeping things tidy and clean. When the meeting is over, stand up and leave when the male students do.

Avoid taking notes. Be tough when the silence comes after the leader says, "Who will record?" When directly asked to do this task, I simply say that I cannot type (this is true) or that I do not have time to get the notes out to everyone.

Avoid learning to type well. Every doctoral student needs to do some typing during the graduate period, if for no other reason than to save money. But being an excellent typist means you will be asked to "help" those who cannot type. Everyone knows that white males cannot type and that all women can. After all, women had to be prepared for a career during high school.

Avoid doing handwork in the presence of colleagues. The benefit of relaxation and enjoyment that comes from working on that needlepoint or afghan does not override the disadvantage of being seen in the conventional female, homemaker role. Just relax and attend to the action of the meeting.

Avoid modifying statements with "I think" or "seemingly" when conducting business. Business is business, and worrying about being too harsh is not part of it. If you sound incompetent and weak, you will be treated that way. Do not apologize for the statement before you even make it.

Avoid the "sweet" image like the plague. This includes mannerisms such as always smiling, always nodding agreement, refusing to take a strong stand, wearing "sweet" clothes (Molloy, 1977), and using a "sweet" tone of voice when intending to sound firm.

Avoid the "flighty" image. This includes mannerisms such as getting off the topic of discussion before it is completed, giggling, and deliberately avoiding conflict or confrontation. If one is thinking seriously, one should act seriously.

Avoid wearing sexy clothes. Molloy's The Woman's Dress for Success Book elaborates upon this idea. His work is based on research. I have found his advice most useful: it works.

Avoid going to the opposite extreme. There is a difference between being feminine and acting unprofessional. Some women lose sight of their female identity. They buy into the white male system with even greater force and commitment than white males. These women never smile, even at appropriate times. They are always very serious; there are times to be businesslike and times not to be. Be able to laugh. Do not take yourself too seriously. Do not start thinking of the opposite sex as the enemy. The richness of the female experience is worth maintaining. The objective is not to become a white male. The objective is to be able to function effectively in a white male society.

Avoid getting caught in the women's lib trap. Many educated white males find it entertaining to tease women about women's liberation issues. I just do not respond to this kind of conversation because it is boring. This ends the joke. It is not worth my energy to be the butt of a joke. On the other hand, I do not hesitate to confront men who are pondering basic issues in a serious way.

Avoid apologizing. Women say "excuse me" and "I'm sorry" way out of proportion to necessity. I have even caught myself apologizing to a chair I bumped into. In the past, I have apologized without even thinking. I no longer do.

Avoid expecting chivalrous behavior from males. If you sit in the car and wait for him to walk around to open your door or if you hold your cigarette and wait for him to light it, you are reinforcing the helpless image. On the other hand, when a male is trying to be kind to you, do not slap him in the face with verbal abuse. The expectation for men to play this role is what I avoid.

Avoid hiding, using nonverbal behaviors. Keep your hands away from your face; do not cover your mouth with your hand. Women typically try to take up only a small space, often sitting in a crumpled position. Spread out. Act confident.

Avoid grooming yourself in public. Keep your hands away from your hair. Your skirt should not be tight enough to need to be pulled down.

Shake hands firmly, but not harshly. The handshake is traditionally the first ritual encounter between two professionals.

During a meeting, sit still and listen. I have done some observation of men in power as they sit at meetings. They do not wiggle or shift positions very often. Sitting still in a relaxed pose gives an aura of attending.

Use direct eye contact. Consciously keep your eyes away from the papers on the seminar table. Look at the speaker. Look at your audience when you are speaking. When walking, consciously keep your eyes away from the ground. Have a look around.

Enlist the help of a tutor. Many of us are married to successful men who are experts at the game. Many of us have male friends or professors who would be willing to coach us if asked. Ask them.

IDENTIFYING MALES WHO ARE
NOT GENDER OBSESSED

The greatest strength women have on campus is other women. Finding or creating female support structures is the theme of another chapter in this book (see Chapter 7). I will focus here on identifying men who can help women in professional growth.

Many men have helped me to become what I am today. To these I have a great debt. When I asked them for help on a particular problem, they responded graciously. They responded to me based on merit and human kindness, disregarding my gender.

Once retired, men often give up some of the white male game. Usually, by age 65, the outstanding men have won the game and have chosen not to play it any longer. Another factor is that these men, who are often grandfathers, are not afraid of some of their own qualities that society has traditionally labeled feminine. They are free to judge a student by merit only. Most of the men who have helped me fit into this category.

The professors who are able and willing to help women students become known to the female student population. By listening to what other women are saying about their professors, one can identify those who are not gender obsessed. For example, one might hear another describing a male professor as "Taking me from where I am," "Able to help me to do the work I want to do, not his work," or "Encouraging me to publish the methodology I used in my dissertation, because he thinks it is an important contribution." The special male professors being described in these statements are interested only in helping each student achieve the most she or he can, regardless of gender.

Finally, it should be noted that there are gender-obsessed women who can be even more harmful to women than some men. For example, one unmarried woman professor got mad because two of her doctoral students refused jobs at major institutions. Both students were married. The professor concluded that married women with preschool children should be blocked from admission to the doctoral program because they would not feel free to move when graduated. Her policy is unofficial, of course. But she cannot be stopped as easily as a man.*

FEMALE ROLE MODELS

Finding a female role model in a predominantly white male institution is a treasure. Since the sample of female professors is small to begin with, identifying a woman who matches one's style of operation and fits one's projection of what one would like to be in the future is a rare occurrence. For me, such a woman would have to be professionally productive, professionally respected, very creative, at ease with her own femininity, able to teach me new modes of operation, and also be kind.

In my graduate experience, it was easier for me to identify female students who could provide me with help, answer my questions, provide insights into the doctoral experience, and listen than to identify a female professorial model or mentor.

SEXUAL RELATIONSHIPS

I had developed a year-long friendship with a male doctoral student. We had been in many classes together. We had rigorously confronted many profes-

---

*That relationships between female students and female faculty members are complicated was found by Hartnett (Katz and Hartnett, 1976, p. 70).

sors in a scholarly manner. After one such confrontation, as we left the room, he patted my behind. The anger rose in me. I was mad because I had assumed a platonic, mutually respectful relationship. With one move, he had tried to change the tenor of that relationship. If I had had any sexual interest in him, my feelings might have been different. He was very embarrassed when I confronted him on this event. Apparently, he had just assumed that a woman would appreciate being patted on the rump. It was obvious that he did not have the desire or capacity to understand what he had done to offend me.

There are often sexual overtones to male-female relationships. The problem comes when these are not mutually desired, when one of the parties is operating on the assumption that a purely nonsexual relationship exists, when the overtones block progress on a desired task, or when they offend one of the parties.

Gossip is another problem female students must cope with. Gossip about women and their sexual behavior, whether based on fact or fiction, travels quickly through many predominantly male faculties. This type of gossip might occur solely on the basis of the woman's beauty. I know of a female student who was so outstanding that she threatened a group of novice male professors. Rumors were started about her sexual promiscuity. The rumors had no factual basis. They made her life miserable. First she gave up her job so that she would no longer have to work with these men. She finally dropped out of the full-time doctoral program and has been struggling to finish her dissertation since. The efforts of these white males worked to remove her from competition with them.

I have no objection to sexual relationships to which both parties mutually consent. I do object to women being viewed as objects for sex first and foremost. I also object to the assumption made by many white males that it is acceptable to impose sexual overtones on all relationships with women, regardless of individual differences. Male professors sometimes subtly (and sometimes not so subtly) connect school success to having sex with them. On one occasion, when I thought a professor was questioning me to get to know me in a teacher-student capacity, he asked if I was living with anyone or if I was available. If every woman who walks into a male professor's office is surveyed as a bedmate, the female student is obviously at a disadvantage. She is a stereotype before she even gets through the door.

My graduate student experience is now over. I came out of it a whole and happy professional despite the forces and factors delineated in this chapter. I attribute this success to my own inherent capacities, to my own stubbornness, to the support of my husband and close female friends, and to those special professors, both female and male, who provided me with new knowledge, skills, attitudes, and experiences. All these factors wielded enough power to get me through the white male institution.

REFERENCES

Gilligan, Carol. "Woman's Place in Man's Life Cycle." Harvard Educational Review 49 (November 1979):431–46.

Katz, Joseph, and Hartnett, Rodney T., eds. Scholars in the Making: The Development of Graduate and Professional Students. Cambridge, Mass.: Ballinger, 1976.

Molloy, John T. The Woman's Dress for Success Book. New York: Warner Books, 1977.

Schaef, Anne Wilson. "It's Not Necessary to Deny Another's Reality in Order to Affirm Your Own—The Systematization of Dualism in the White Male Structure." First National Conference on Human Relations in Education, Minneapolis, Minnesota, June 21, 1978.

6

NEW BRAINS FOR OLD BODIES: THE IMPACT OF EMOTIONAL AND PHYSICAL STRESS DURING THE PH.D. PROCESS

Sharon Barnett

"Is the Ph.D. worth the process?" she asked. "No!"
I answered. "Not at this point in time." For me the
cost both physically and emotionally was too high.
Presently with all but the dissertation (A.B.D.) completed, I view the process at age 43 as costly because
of my age, a geographical move, and leaving an excellent administrative position. In another year with
the completed degree in hand and, I hope, a fulfilling
position, I may say, "Yes, I did this for myself, for
who I am, and just perhaps, because of a Ph.D. new
doors will be opened!"

It was summer. The red ridges of the Rockies stretched before me on a clear, dry afternoon in early August. I had come to
the familiar resort town in Colorado to visit my aunt and uncle and
to renew an exhausted body, a confused mind, and a restless spirit.
My aunt and I sat sipping lemonade and breaking fresh green beans
from her garden. The silence—one of a longtime friendship, a comfort of kindred spirits, and a knowingness that can come only with
time—was finally broken.
　　With love and a confidence in her own perception and wisdom,
she looked at me intently and finally said: "My dear, this is the
first time I can remember since you were a young child that you did
not seem to have a cause to justify. It is so pleasant just being with
you! Do you know what you want? Is this Ph.D. program what you
need? You seem so exhausted from this past year of study. You
are 42 years old—still very attractive and so intelligent. You've
had a lot of unhappiness in your personal life—the divorce, raising

three children on your own. I think I know you Sharon. I think I know how much you want and need to share your life with someone, but I also know your quick, searching mind, your need to be intensely involved in your work—your often singleness of purpose. Is the Ph.D. the answer?"

Simple questions! How insightful this woman, my aunt! How quietly but perceptively she had been watching me these past few days as I had soaked in the warm sun, the quiet of their lovely home nestled near the river in trees and pasture land. Here I had a feeling of belonging, of the familiar, of a simpler, direct, less complicated style of life.

How could so much happen in just one year? The first year in the Ph.D. program at Ohio State University had been a year of multiple adjustments. So many changes in my life pattern—too many changes—falling under the popular labels of "midlife transition," "critical life events," "empty nest syndrome," "role-identity crisis," and "reentry." My decision to enter a Ph.D. program at midlife had meant a major geographical move, resigning my position as a college administrator, leaving two sons on the West Coast, and separating from family and friends.

Now at the end of that first year of change I had found the time to sit and reflect upon just what changes and adjustments were involved in entering the program. The cost had been high in terms of emotional and physical distress. Emotionally I felt separated from family and friends. I had to build a new support system. The intensity of study in a doctoral program leaves little time for a social life or to cultivate relationships other than those among fellow graduate students. The financial adjustment of coming from a full-time position to a half-time research or teaching assignment can impact all phases of one's life, including housing, nutrition, socialization, and recreation. A homeowner can become an apartment dweller. Membership in the tennis or swim club is no longer possible for most students. The temptation to turn to fast foods rather than take the time to prepare and eat a well-balanced, varied diet is a common practice. Never having worn glasses I was surprised that, after just a few months of intense study and eyestrain, I needed glasses for reading. The body, in an attempt to adjust or rebel against the strain of the program and the long hours of work and study, often finds a target organ that gives symptoms that are stress related. During my first year of study, an ongoing vascular condition known as Raynaud's Disease was rediagnosed as a nonprogressive form of a more serious collagen disease that I am certain is stress related.

As I was able to share my own concern about my emotional and physical stress reactions with my peers, I became increasingly aware of what seemed to be an inordinate amount of emotional and physical problems among the other research and teaching associates I encountered. The symptoms fell into categories including skin irritations, headaches, gastrointestinal disorders, and reproductive organ irregularities (such as irregular menstrual cycles not experienced prior to the program).

In "Emotional Problems of the Graduate Student," Seymour Halleck suggests that it is possible to consider maladaptive behavior by examining the manner in which an individual seeks to satisfy two basic needs: the need for meaningful activity and the need for intimacy. Whether these needs are gratified or frustrated depends upon a person's biological strengths and weaknesses and the social circumstances in which that person finds herself.

Most people enter the Ph.D. process feeling that they will receive gratification for their efforts. A person who chooses such a commitment for a three-year period is already a high achiever. Such an individual puts an internal structure of high expectations upon herself, and yet is the type of person who turns to authorities within education (such as professors, researchers, authors) as her standard for success. After all, she has learned to play the academic game par excellence,* and has been rewarded by her past endeavors to consider a terminal degree in her field.

However, upon entering the doctoral program, the outstanding student now finds that she is only one among the cream of the crop. Doctoral students often enter a program for advancement within a system and after they have held respectable positions within or outside the university setting. To take on the role of graduate student may quickly lead to a feeling of prolonged frustration rather than gratification. Course work is often tailored to the expertise of the instructor rather than to the point of development of the student. Teaching and research assignments are often given on a reward basis for services to professors or the department that are not directly related to the area of strength or expertise of the student. Both the general exam process and the dissertation can be designed to meet the research needs of a committee member or a department commitment rather than serving as a foundation for the student's future professional interest or academic thrust. Many advisers, committee members, and other faculty can offer the support and sensitivity necessary to make the process one of gratification of specific skills and abilities, so that prolonged frustration does not build over a period of time to symptoms of emotional and physical stress.

---

*But perhaps has more to learn (see Chapter 5).

Stress-related illnesses are linked to the number of changes over a specific amount of time, as well as to the continuation of a specific circumstance or frustration over which the person has little or no control. Entering the doctoral program means many changes in living patterns over a short period of time. Most first-year students find themselves scoring in the critical area on the Holmes and Rahe inventory of critical life events.[1] This inventory lists major changes that can occur in living patterns and gives a numerical value to each. Entering a doctoral program often means a major geographical relocation, a change in financial status, a new residence, separation from family and friends, the establishing of new relationships, as well as a new work assignment, to mention only some major scoring items. Many students enter the program during an ongoing life transition. A return to the closed environment of the campus can serve as a false security following the death of a spouse, a separation or divorce, a lonely home with the children grown and gone, the loss of a position or the desire to change life goals professionally, or the search for a last challenge in midlife. For such "seekers," the entering of a program may hold the gratification desired, but for others frustration may result. The combination of multiple changes and ongoing frustration sets the doctoral student up for stress, which may affect physical and emotional health.

Although the need for intimacy is always present, for the doctoral student long-standing support systems may change or may no longer be feasible due to the demands of the program. The greatest source of support often comes from other graduate students who are sharing the intense process. Family, friends, spouses, and children may be at a geographical distance. The foreign student is especially likely to fall victim to this item of stress. Both foreign students and older students (over 40) may experience additional problems in establishing a new support system (see Chapter 10). There is often a need for an intimate relationship with another person (see Chapter 8). "Those makers and breakers" (those entering or exiting from an intimate relationship) are already experiencing stressful periods. The results associated with the isolation or withdrawal of an abstainer (one choosing not to enter into an emotional involvement), as well as the stressful complications that might occur when a sexual relationship develops between a professor and student, are obvious.

Because of the research in stress, which consumed much of my time and interest my first year of study, and my own coping patterns with physical and emotional stress, I decided to survey my fellow graduate students concerning their health problems and stress symptoms during the doctoral process. I developed a two-page form and circulated it among Ph.D. students in the college of education at

Ohio State University. Responses included students in early and middle childhood, foundations and research, teacher education, educational communication, and educational administration. The returned forms included the responses of 30 students. These students ranged from the first year of study completed through completion of the degree and job placement. I found very few patterns. Physical and emotional illness and coping systems were as individual as the person involved. There was a slight tendency for an increase in health problems in the second and third year of study. However, one male student in administration reported a tremendous improvement in overall health since entering the program. His wife, also a Ph.D. student, reported major health problems had developed during her second year of study. The question might arise as to the impact of male/female role identity and the stress of graduate study. Students with recurring or chronic problems often saw such problems as stress related.

An unusual problem among female graduate students was reported by three students in their late twenties or early thirties. These three young women, all married, had "endometriosis," which is the presence of endometrial tissue in abnormal locations, as in the uterine wall. Each of the women acknowledged that this problem might well be stress related, and one mentioned that her physician had suggested this relationship. The condition of this foreign tissue often renders sterility. Another female student developed large uterine tumors during her second year of study, which limited the time available for childbearing. Questions arise as to how such a condition relates to women who have postponed childbearing due to a professional commitment and to what extent such a condition is related to a role conflict over motherhood versus professionalism. Studies relating female conflicts over role identity have been prominent in looking at suicides in female doctors. [2] Many female doctoral students compete with men and yet still feel they must fulfill the traditional female role to be adequate. The stress often takes a physical as well as an emotional toll.

There was an overall agreement among the students surveyed that financial adjustment during the first year of the program caused the most concern and stress. The single most stressful period of time within the three-year period was the quarter in preparation for the comprehensive examination and the taking of the examination (see Chapter 3). Physical symptoms during this time included intestinal disorders, skin rashes, weight gain (20 pounds were reported gained by several women), irregular menstrual cycles, nervousness, and lack of sleep.

An ongoing support system for the doctoral student is essential to survival (see Chapter 7). The most consistent support mentioned by female students was that of other female graduate students in the program. Males mentioned spouses or parents more frequently. Female students mentioned spouses or children following the consistent support of other female students. Relations with other faculty members and the adviser varied from excellent to adequate to inconsistent to nonexistent. Inconsistent support of the adviser was frequently mentioned.

Major changes in the personal lives of graduate students varied. For some the loss of a relative, a divorce, or change in living environment affected health. For others it was only an "adjustment" period. The death of a female graduate student due to a car accident was mentioned the most frequently as the cause of several weeks of emotional distress among female students. Not only friendship, but also role identity within the program was affected by this loss. Both associates and faculty serving on the same project as the deceased student were acutely aware of the impact of this loss on them personally and on the time line of the project. Other students became aware that all intense effort can be swept away in an instant. Students also gained a new awareness of the young woman's contributions to groups outside of the university. Doctoral candidates have a tendency to relate to one another only in the role designated by the contact in the program.

Few students showed a balance of activities in their lives. The majority of the students did not participate regularly in physical, spiritual, social, or nonacademic activities. Reading for pleasure and television viewing varied from one extreme to the other. Married students tended to have more friendships outside the program and to participate more in nonacademic groups. Single students tended to center almost all contacts within the program.

Support services were often unavailable or inadequate for three special groups of graduate students: the foreign student, who tended to be isolated and extremely involved in academic studies; the older married student (over 40), who centered more time around family or spouse; and the single older student, who, if female, was often involved with children or other commitments outside the program.

I returned to my second year in the program with a new and more realistic understanding of the demands, stresses, and systems for coping to survive in an intense, competitive environment. I made some very specific decisions concerning activities and relationships. I made time regularly for physical activity—for me that meant prioritizing money to join an indoor tennis club, but also it meant taking advantage of courses in theatrical dance available as part of my regular tuition expense at the university. I also spent more time nurturing relationships with both male and female friends who were completely unconnected with the university—a really fresh perspective. I made time for pleasure reading. For me spiritual renewal meant active participation in a peer-counseling group at my church. Both my physical and emotional health took on new vitality. In the spring I took my general exams with a feeling of a positive accomplishment through sharing my academic interests with my committee in writing and orally. For me there was no "postgenerals depression" (see Chapter 3). I immediately tackled the writing of the dissertation proposal.

The key to maintaining physical and emotional health during the doctoral process seems to center around developing and maintaining an adequate support system, and maintaining a physiopsychosocial balance of meaningful activities. My own experience, as well as the information shared with me by other students, leads me to generalize and make a few recommendations for survival during the process.

- Be aware of and prepare adequately for the financial change, which is a definite handicap during the program.
- Put the degree in the proper perspective. You are you, with or without the degree.
- Keep social contacts both inside and outside the program. There are people in the world without Ph.D.s or who do not care if you or they have the degree.
- Seek professional or personal counseling early, if needed.
- Find or maintain a personal support system including friends, spouse, children, and parents.
- Keep a record of the number of changes that are occurring in your life over a six-month period. For each new change find a balance for more time, energy, and support.
- If appropriate, fight to take the general exam pressure out of your program. What are the alternatives (for example, project, article, test taken over several quarters, test taken in a private room, take oral exam only)? Change the test to fit your style. You take control. Be the maker and director of your fate.
- Balance your activities, including daily physical, spiritual, social, and recreational time. Yes, daily! It is possible. By attending to the above you will complete the Ph.D. program with a strong, healthy body under that great brain, as well as a glowing spirit surrounding it.

NOTES

1. R. H. Rahe, "The Pathway between Subject's Recent Life Changes and Their Near-Future Illness Reports," in B. Dohrenwend

and B. Dohrenwend, eds., Stressful Life Events: Their Nature and Effects (New York: Wiley, 1974).

2. W. Archibald, "Stress Causes Suicide among Female Doctors," Ohio State Lantern, May 25, 1979.

BIBLIOGRAPHY

Archibald, W. "Stress Causes Suicide among Female Doctors." Ohio State Lantern, May 25, 1979.

Beehr, T. A., and Schuler, R. S. "Current and Future Perspectives on Job Stress in Organizations," in K. Rowland and G. Ferris (Eds.), Personnel Management: New Perspectives. Boston: Allyn and Bacon, in press.

Frankenhaeuser, M., and Gardell, B. "Underload and Overload in Working Life." Outline of a multidisciplinary approach. Journal of Human Stress, 1976, 2, 35-45.

Halleck, Seymour L. "Emotional Problems of the Graduate Student," in Joseph Katz and Rodney T. Hartnett (Eds.), Scholars in the Making: The Development of Graduate and Professional Students. Cambridge, JA: Ballinger, 1976.

Lakein, A. How to Get Control of Your Time and Your Life. New York: Signet, 1973.

Lazarus, R. S. "Cognitive and Personality Factors Underlying Threat and Coping," in Sol Levine and Norman A. Scotch (Eds.), Social Stress. Chicago: Aldine, 1970.

_____. Psychological Stress and the Coping Process. New York: McGraw-Hill, 1966.

Lefcourt, H. M. Locus of Control. Hillsdale, N.J.: Lawrence Erlbaum Associates, 1976.

Levi, L. Stress and Distress in Response to Psychosocial Stimuli. Elinsford, N.J.: Pergamon, 1972.

Levinson, D. J. "The Mid-Life Transition: A Period in Adult Psychosocial Development," Psychiatry, 1977, 40, 99-112.

Pellitier, K. Mind as Healer, Mind as Slayer. New York: Dell, 1976.

Rahe, R. H. "The Pathway between Subject's Recent Life Changes and Their Near-Future Illness Reports," in B. Dohrenwend and B. Dohrenwend (Eds.) Stressful Life Events: Their Nature and Effects. New York: Wiley, 1974.

Rotter, J. B. "Generalized Expectancies for Internal versus External Control of Reinforcement," Psychological Monographs, 1966, 80.

Selye, H. The Stress of Life. New York: McGraw-Hill, 1956.

_____. Stress Without Distress. New York: Signet, 1974.

Stress. Blue Cross Association, Chicago, 1974.

7

THE DIARY OF A WEB SPINNER

Katherine O. Tracey

This account of the development of a female support
network is based on my personal experience. Support networks have provided me and my sister web
spinners with practical information and emotional
nourishment throughout our graduate experience.
Now that I have my Ph.D., I find that networks continue to enhance my professional life.

Spiders spin webs to survive. Those geometric structures of
sticky filaments have amazing suppleness and strength. They help
provide their spinners with nourishment and protection. People
spin the webs of a support network for similar reasons. Within such
a strong yet flexible human web, people can find informational and
emotional nourishment.

Curious children have often asked, "How does a spider learn
to spin its web?" The usual answer is, "I'm not sure. They just
seem to know." A person entering a doctoral program may ask the
same question. "How can I spin a human support web to find nourishment and safety in these new surroundings?" The answer is
often, "I'm not sure how. Students just seem to know."

The following is my answer to that "how" question by sharing
a personal account of how one woman doctoral candidate spun a web
of support and was well nourished by it. The steps in this web-
spinning process seem obvious in retrospect. They are shared
here as a case study or model for those of you to follow since they
were so significant in my graduate school experience.

WOMEN ARE EXPERIENCED WEB SPINNERS

We women moving in increasing numbers out of full-time roles as homemakers, have often ignored our need for establishing support networks. We have accepted the stereotype promoted by cartoons and sitcoms that neighborhood gatherings and women's clubs represent wasted, unproductive time.

In Marilyn French's The Women's Room (1977), the reader follows Mira from her early adulthood in a small suburban neighborhood through her experiences 20 years later as a graduate student. The book focuses on the support networks in which she is involved in both settings. The women in Mira's neighborhood provided each other with support as they struggled with the many challenges of raising young children, making ends meet on limited incomes, and confronting shattered dreams and broken promises. They provided support, not solutions.

When I was a child my family lived in a neighborhood that resembled Mira's. I grew up with a valuable model because my mother and the other women in our neighborhood were part of a mutually supportive network. They shared their skills, thoughts, joys, and concerns. Being homemakers was important, and these supportive relationships were significant to the women who created them.

Establishing genuine relationships that can develop into a support network takes time. For women at home this might be an informal gathering or might be talking while the children play in the yard. For business people this might be over coffee or at a business club lunch (a practice that is often exclusively male). For university people this might be at lunch, or chatting after a faculty meeting. In any case, it involves a personal outreach and a sincere sharing.

This is not to say that every shared cup of coffee, every conversation, or every lunch is immediately productive or will lead to establishing a support network. It is a reminder that support networks can grow only as a result of continuing contact and through mutual interests and needs. There is no instant web building for spiders or people. If women accept the stereotype that friendly and informal chats are nonproductive time, then we overlook the important potential of such communication. Women enter new roles outside the home without honoring previous experience in establishing support networks or an acknowledgment of the significance of such relationships.

Spiders know instinctively how to spin webs, and yet for people the analogy of spider webs and support networks breaks down here. Many students do not seem to have an instinctive ability to establish a human support system within the university, nor do they recognize its importance.

In The Women's Room as Mira left her marriage and suburban life and returned to graduate school, she felt frightened and alone. She did not recognize her own potential, nor did she understand her need to be a part of a support system. Many of us shared Mira's feelings of being alone and on the outside of a mysterious system as we entered our doctoral programs. The Women's Room describes the relationships Mira developed with her fellow students. A group of women graduate students formed the core of this network, and they supported each other by sharing needs, experiences, ideas, feelings, and resources. Through trial and error, Mira and her friends discovered the strength possible when working as a team.

WOMEN ARE RAISED NOT KNOWING THE VALUE OF TEAM BUILDING

In their book The Managerial Woman, Margaret Hennig and Anne Jardim describe the different mind-sets of executive females and males; their assumptions, perceptions, and behavior. Many of the distinctions the authors found could be traced back to childhood and patterns of play. These patterns provide an additional clue as to why women have overlooked the significance of a support network.

Much early male play is centered on athletics and team sports:

> A team makes it possible to become a star and one has
> to learn how to manage this. A team makes it possible
> to share a star's luster by active association and again
> one can learn how to manage this. A team can even be
> a place to hide, a place to learn about survival—how to
> stay on, how to be given another chance; "after all,
> he's too nice a guy to drop!", or "he's really not pro-
> ducing yet but he's learning fast, and he's a real
> straight player!" Over and above this, there is the
> drive to win and of the necessity to win as a team,
> not as a lone individual independent of everyone else.
> (Hennig and Jardim, 1977, p. 41)

A team's interdependency, which is necessary for one's personal survival, is an experience for which most girls have no parallel:

> The prestigious sports for girls tend to be one-on-
> one; tennis, swimming, golf, gymnastics, skating.

> And in one-on-one sports, the old adage that "it's
> not whether you won or lost but how you play the
> game" has been stressed so that many women tennis
> players now in their twenties still play for "exer-
> cise—they don't play to win." (Hennig and Jardim,
> 1977, p. 45)

Thus the way children participate in sports and the goals of those sports distinctly varies between males and females.

It can be argued that a person's career and the academic preparation for it are merely other types of play. If this is true, then women and men "play" at their work and academic preparation differently. Men intuitively grasp the importance of team building, where women may feel that personal effort and achievement is of greatest value.

MY WEB SPINNING: A SUPPORT
NETWORK IN PROCESS

I had been a graduate student on a part-time basis for over six years before taking the plunge and entering a full-time doctoral program. I did not expect things to be very different. That was the first false assumption. All of a sudden the challenges of having to develop a program, declare areas of major concentration, form a committee, and begin preparing for the qualifying general exams became complicated issues. I had entered the doctoral program feeling very confident and competent. Now I felt very naive and alone. Where to begin? Who could answer my questions? How could I learn to play this game? I was surprised to discover that being a capable student was not enough.

The university advisement system was the prescribed com-munication network for graduate students. For me that system only provided partial information and little support in my struggle to learn how to play the female graduate student game. I soon learned that significant information was communicated informally from stu-dent to student. This network carried the information about courses and professors that greatly broadened the descriptions in the col-lege catalog. It increased my awareness of options within programs and offered practical suggestions about forming my committee and expanding professional horizons. I was learning a valuable lesson about the contrasts in formal and informal communication. To par-ticipate in an informal network required contact and time to talk with my fellow students.

During that first winter more than the weather was gloomy. I was enrolled in a course in my major area of concentration and found myself feeling less and less adequate as the quarter progressed. My tests and papers were returned with an abundance of criticism. The class lectures seemed to emphasize how much students did not know. I was unable to determine which of my ideas were good and which needed to be developed or discarded. These were new frustrations for me, and throughout most of the quarter I struggled alone. I remember feeling that if I tried a little harder I would finally succeed. That was the second false assumption.

Near the end of that quarter I risked sharing my feelings with some other students. To my amazement, these men and women were also experiencing frustrations. We decided to mark the end of winter quarter by meeting for lunch—a celebration of survival! By coincidence, only the women came for lunch. Without realizing it, we took our first step in establishing a women's support network.

During that next summer we began meeting every week for lunch. Our only formal structure was to establish the time and place. Some of us came every week; other women came only occasionally. We began inviting other female graduate students to share what was fast becoming a most special time of sharing.

As fall quarter approached most of us made plans to return to busier schedules of working as graduate assistants and being full-time doctoral students, so we made a commitment to meet only once a month for lunch. The pleasure and support of sharing joys and struggles with other women had become very important to all of us. We found that our loosely structured "lunch bunch" had been transformed into a cohesive support group. Our shared interests and needs added to the enrichment we found in our diversity of majors, life-styles, and ages.

We informally adopted our own rituals, such as meeting for extra lunchtime relaxers when someone was writing general exams or celebrating after an oral defense. Those women who had completed one academic stage shared their advice and insights with those of us who followed. In a predominantly male institution we became each other's role models and helped build linkages to the professional world to follow.

Graduation marked a special time for celebration, but it changed the nature and needs of our group. Meeting on campus for lunch was no longer possible for the women who had moved into outside professional roles. Yet the need for sharing with other women and the support our group provided had not changed; so our setting became a monthly supper gathering in each other's homes. The topics changed from student-oriented issues to those profession-oriented issues of finding job opportunities, writing for professional journals, presenting at conferences, or coordinating research with full-time work.

Our group is now scattered, and we could provide a most interesting national and international tour. We cannot share the monthly supper celebrations, but we can still participate in the support network through occasional telephone calls, a round-robin letter, and by meetings at national conferences. We continue to provide both personal and professional support by sharing research, working together on writing projects and presentations, and informing each other of job opportunities. We continue to share the joys and challenges of being women in predominantly male settings.

MY ADVICE TO WEB SPINNERS

As web spinners it is important not to ignore the potential of informal communication. Meeting for lunch after a frustrating quarter grew into a most significant influence on my academic and professional growth. The key ingredients in developing a support network are to take time to communicate with other people and to risk sharing. The web cannot be made unless there are supports on which to attach it. An informal group will develop only if members have common interests and needs. Unless we communicate and share ourselves, we never know what we have in common. In almost any setting (university, office, neighborhood, or factory) we can create an environment in which a support network can develop.

First, think about what you need. As women have entered more business, professional, and academic roles, we have begun to recognize the need for support from other women. Within the university setting, I needed support in the challenges of combining my roles of mother, wife, and student (see Chapter 9). I also needed to understand the university system and to expand my professional horizons.

Second, look for individuals with whom you share needs and interests and arrange to be with those people. Having recognized the general need for support from other women, women's networks are being organized in many communities. In my community this involves an open invitation given to interested women who wish to meet once a month. This network is not a club, nor does it have a formal program. It addresses the need for women to share concerns and experiences, to celebrate and support each other, and to gain from their similarities and diversities.

This type of networking is vitally important. In assuming new roles, women have been limited to traditional formal communication routes. We have overlooked those wonderful networks men have established in the business, professional, and academic world. Women's networks begin to address this need.

Third, be patient with the process. Just creating the environment does not guarantee creating the desired support network. It takes much patience to be a web spinner. Relationships develop over time and require mutual commitment. In our networking process, some women who came to lunch and seemed to enjoy our group chose not to come regularly. Perhaps their needs and resources were different. After that first summer, a core group of "regulars" emerged.

Meeting for lunch is not a magic formula, but if you make no attempt to create an environment in which meeting other people and communicating can occur, no support network will develop.

In "Research on Women in Educational Leadership Roles," presented by Jacqueline P. Clement at A.S.C.D. National Conference (St. Louis, Missouri, March 8, 1981), Dr. Clement described four things women need to do in order to increase opportunities in leadership roles:

1. Women need to support other women.
2. Women need to encourage other women to be in the application pool. We often feel we need to be perfectly prepared before applying for a position.
3. Women need to be allowed to fail without experiencing guilt.
4. Women must insist that feedback is task oriented rather than person oriented (i.e., women are often told how to improve appearance rather than performance).

I was sitting with one of my graduate school friends as I listened to Jackie Clement's excellent presentation. I realized so clearly how our women's support network had touched all four of those areas. We had supported and encouraged each other in many professional and personal ways. We had struggled together to be authentic people dealing with successes and failures. We had provided each other with task-oriented feedback and had planned strategies for receiving more such feedback from the male-dominated system. I also reflected upon how much each of us had grown during the four years since our first celebration lunch.

Networking requires time and commitment. Contrary to the spider analogy, knowledge of spinning the web of a human support group is not instinctive. My web spinning had to be learned, but it is now an ongoing process. New webs are added as new circumstances and needs arise. Old webs need to be attended. Our original women's support network continued to evolve to match our expanding professional experiences and changing locations.

We can learn a valuable lesson from the spider. Webs are spun with purpose. They must be strong yet flexible. Such webs can capture unexpected treasures.

REFERENCES

Clement, Jacqueline P. "Research on Women in Educational Leadership Roles." A.S.C.D. National Conference, St. Louis, March 8, 1981.

French, Marilyn. The Women's Room. New York: Summit Books, 1977.

Hennig, Margaret, and Jardim, Anne. The Managerial Woman. New York: Simon and Schuster, 1977.

8

IN AND OUT OF RELATIONSHIPS: A SERIOUS GAME FOR THE WOMAN DOCTORAL STUDENT

Rosalind Williams

We met in a stairwell. She said, "We're organizing
a group to write a book on women and doctoral study."

"That sounds great," I replied. "You know, you
should consider including some ideas on women and
their relationships during graduate school." Following
my comment, I was promptly nominated.

For me the interviewing and thinking associated
with this project have had personal benefits as I re-
examined my own experience and came to understand
myself and others more completely. Only today I realize that I have spent much of my life looking for someone who would take better care of me than I could. I
just may have to admit that I'm the best person for the
job.

If women are indeed taking on new roles, then one of them
must certainly be that of juggler. This comparison cannot be new to
many working women; however, it does seem to pose some special
problems for the woman who studies at the doctoral level. Each
woman chooses to juggle a slightly different set of objects. Some
sets that seem common to many doctoral students are study and
intellectual development, professional interactions, building support
groups, maintaining family ties, and the development and nurturance
of intimate relationships. This last object to juggle appears to be
highly significant to many of us, both because of its basic importance
to our existence, and because it often seems to be the one object that
threatens to tumble to the ground as we attempt to keep all our other
objects in the air.

This chapter will be an examination of some of my and other women's ideas about the performance of that juggling act, particularly as it concerns the topic of intimate relationships. It was reported that a male professor's comment to a woman discussing the formation of her doctoral program and confessing that she had just been divorced was, "Well, you've fulfilled the first prerequisite to doctoral study." It has been observed by professors and students alike that the incidence of divorce and other relationship disturbance before, during, and after doctoral programs seems very high. This may simply represent a subgroup of a larger societal trend; however, at times it would appear that there are some special considerations relevant to the female doctoral student. There seem to be several distinct relationship modes that female doctoral students pursue. In addition, specific behaviors within these modes are highly varied.

It is a popular notion that the important issues in women's lives center around relationships, whereas significant concerns to men are more related to their achievements. Some women have railed against this sort of generalization, while others have argued that we need to recognize that there may be such a difference and we should work in harmony with it rather than try to negate it. After studying the literature of child development, Gilligan (1979) writes of her growing conviction that women do focus more of their energy on the development and nurturance of relationships with others. She says that this basic difference proceeds from the ways that boys and girls are reared in their very early years and the ways in which they come to identify themselves. Women typically remain in strong relationships with their mothers, while boys are encouraged to differentiate and move away from that bond much earlier. Gilligan sees the result not as a pathological lack of individuation as proposed by some Freudian theorists, but rather an adjustment to the balance of life that places greater emphasis on relationships and cooperative ventures throughout life. As pointed out in other chapters of this volume (see Chapter 5), this different style of balancing relationships and achievements may cause difficulties in a woman's progress toward a doctoral degree. It would seem that it might place added stress on the way a woman arranges her most intimate relationships as well.

Erikson's eight stages of man (1963) are generally helpful in understanding the process of human development, but the theory also points to a difference in women's growth toward maturity. During adolescence and early adulthood, all young people must deal with the life crises of identity and then intimacy. Women, however, sometimes postpone identity formation until they have achieved an intimate relationship. At that time the woman's identity becomes

one with the identity of the intimate person. Beyond the initial resolution, these two developmental tasks remain a conflict for many
women as they sort out how much of their identification comes from
personal qualities and talents and how much through the partner.
When will she be viewed as Dr. Smith-Paige and when Mrs. Paige?
As important as personal identity and intimacy are to all humans,
these seem to be precisely the areas of greatest difficulty for many
contemporary women.

In The Women's Room (1977) and The Bleeding Heart (1980),
Marilyn French described two intriguing female characters who
are, or become, interested in academic pursuits. Mira and Delores
both have great difficulty in finding the love and support they desire
from relationships with men while maintaining their own identities
as individuals and scholars. French seems to be telling her readers that they must guard themselves carefully against the debilitat-
ing effects of close relationships with men. Otherwise, they may
be completely destroyed personally and lose their capability to
achieve any intellectual goals. The women discussed in this chapter
did not all experience similar levels of distress as did Mira and
Delores, but the basic bind is familiar to many women in academic
life. In response to that conflict, women find many methods of
accommodating their needs and desires while successfully completing doctoral study.

Since there are a number of different styles of intimate relating among women doctoral students, the discussion that follows will
examine women's experiences in four general categories. They are
the makers and breakers of relationships, the daters, the abstainers,
and the sustainers. No claim is made that these categories are all-
inclusive, and it is assumed that some women may fit more than
one category. Typically, however, interviewees readily identified
themselves with one category. A fifth focus discusses briefly the
special situation of intimate relationships with professors. This
topic seemed of particularly critical concern to many women. It
has been suggested that the chapter could include information on
lesbian relationships. Although not dealt with in this chapter, they
are seen as another important variation on the relationship theme.
The women represented herein all indicated that their chosen primary relationships were with men. Therefore, it is these male-
female interactions that are the focus here.

The experiences related in this chapter come from the author's
life, from her own intimates, and from a series of semistructured
interviews conducted with women who were doctoral students or had
recently completed doctoral study. No attempt is made to analyze
the information empirically; rather the goal of this account is to suggest some of the aspects of the relationship contexts of these wom-
en's lives.

THE MAKERS AND BREAKERS OF RELATIONSHIPS

These women could be said to be either very brave or very foolish. They seem to experience several aspects of their lives fully and often plunge ahead into changes without the concern for protecting themselves that some other relationship types express. For one reason or another, these women are risk takers.

A great many women have made some type of relationship change as a prelude to entry into doctoral study. This type of disruption is usually associated with the woman's changing view of herself and her aspirations. If she and her partner are unable to work out some change in their own style of relating, then a break often becomes inevitable. In some cases this has been as a direct result of the woman's desire to continue her education, while other women made this decision to continue study after finding themselves no longer bound by the expectations contained in that earlier relationship. A corollary to that latter type of decision is that the woman is likely to realize that not only does she now have her chance, but she also has become completely responsible for her own livelihood and may need to upgrade her ability to handle that task.

One woman described the precipitous breakup of a long-term engagement that was largely a result of her decision to enter doctoral study. This was a saddening experience for her, but one that she has come to view as inevitable and right for her. Another woman spoke of her divorce after an eight-year marriage. The divorce did not result from a conflict about a decision to attend graduate school, but was the culmination of a mismatch of partner expectations. The husband had pursued his own career through a Ph.D. and into a university teaching position. When the wife began to make relatively small forays toward her own career development, the dissatisfactions on both sides grew until a divorce resulted. This woman then decided to pursue doctoral study, a course that would probably have been impossible within her marriage. These women found the role conflict between being partner and career developer too great to allow continuance of their relationships in spite of their desires for loving and intimacy.

One of the more striking features that characterized the makers and breakers was a certain abandon with which they approached entering new relationships. Not only did they seek out new associations as did the daters, but they also seemed unafraid to pursue these new relationships to their ultimate conclusion—dissolution or permanent liaison. These women met partners in a variety of ways, including bars, sports activities, conference attendance, and mutual friends' introductions. They did not seem to show a great deal of concern for the negative effect that a new relationship could have on their professional development. Apparently this tendency reflects a significant need for these women to fully develop all portions of their lives, sometimes simultaneously.

Another difference noted was that these makers and breakers seemed more likely to become intimately involved with men with quite different life-styles than those found in the academic community. These women also seemed to some extent to compartmentalize their various strivings. During the week they might be the most serious of students, while weekends might be completely devoted to the nurturance of relationships or simply to having fun with their partners. This characteristic is certainly not limited to the makers and breakers, but it did seem to be a strong indicator of the intensity with which they approached each segment of their experience.

Because of this compartmentalization, these women do not seem to have the same requirements for partners described by some other female doctoral students. They are more likely to choose a person for reasons strictly related to the style of interaction and the type of family organization that they perceive to be possible. They are less concerned about their partner's interest in their work and seem to desire acceptance rather than sharing of the career experience. Perhaps that attitude reflects realism gained after wishes for greater support had been unattainable.

Divorce or termination of a long-term relationship has also occurred toward the end of, or immediately following, the doctoral program. This is a very special phenomenon that is similar in nature to the earlier divorces, but is also much more specific. Two women who divorced within a year of graduation could almost be described as emerging from hibernation. They seemed to gain a new sense of self that was affirmed by the completion of the degree. With this affirmation, they took courage and broke out of relationships that they had seen as protective or supportive in some ways, but that did not fit with their new self-images. As these women bloomed, they could not bring their marriages into line with the new expectations. Although the description is of a generally positive trend for these women, the breakups were certainly full of pain and conflict. The step into the world with only a doctoral degree for protection was often experienced as frightening, but was also viewed as finally essential to their self-actualization.

Late breakups might be viewed in another light. These women stayed with a known situation while they were experiencing the great stress of the final stages of doctoral study. When they finished or had the end in sight, they were able to redirect their energies without savoring the protectiveness of the marriage. Both explanations seem valid, but again we see that flash of risk taking.

Intimate relationships are very important to makers and breakers. That may be one reason why they have gathered the courage to end and begin relationships even with the demanding course of doctoral study. In at least some cases they place greater importance on the quality of intimacy than they do on the development of their careers. This fact is demonstrated as women move to new cities for relationships rather than jobs, and postpone or delay graduate study in favor of consolidating new associations. They are willing to take a chance that their own professional satisfaction will be less than the best so that they can be in a relationship that satisfies intimacy needs. Perhaps they are particularly sensitive barometers of the severe pressures that women experience when they attempt to fully develop themselves intellectually, socially, and emotionally. The makers and breakers attack life, sometimes without regard for the short-range consequences, but with faith that somehow they will be able to juggle all those balls—at least for some exciting moments.

THE DATER

Is she a carefree, modern woman who is the envy of all her peers? Could we rename this section "Sex and the Intellectual Female"? The proportion of women doctoral students and recent graduates in this category was surprisingly low. Some abstainers might have liked to be numbered in this group, but they had come to another decision (for their own reasons) that they would not pursue such a life-style. As Katz and Hartnett (1976) point out, the social scene of graduate school is not especially conducive to meeting others who may be interested in forming intimate relationships. The daters with whom I spoke bear out this institutional condition, since they met most of their intimates in work settings away from the university, through friends, or at nonuniversity social functions. Some women even discussed the pitfalls of becoming involved with another student.

Daters have relatively clear reasons for having chosen their particular relationship style. They seem to be confident people who tended to "make things happen" for themselves. They had chosen to date rather than make long-term commitments sometimes because they did not feel they had sufficient time to devote to a marriage or live-in relationship. They were not willing, however, to deny their social, sexual, or intimate friendship needs and desires, so they found dating to be the most satisfactory compromise. One woman also mentioned that she wished to remain mobile and did not want to form a permanent relationship in the same area where she was attending graduate school. These women who are daters during graduate school do not see it as a permanent condition; rather, it is their chosen adaptation to the current demands on their lives.

There were a number of types of dating relationships mentioned by these women. There are the inevitable short-lived one- or two-time dates. An interesting twist with the daters was that they seemed to gain control of such situations, not letting themselves become involved with a one-night stand that they would later regret. One woman mentioned that she used the opportunity of the first couple of dates to assess the possibilities of that relationship, and then made a decision as to whether it would continue or not. There were also friendly dating relationships that might continue over a number of years, with both parties remaining satisfied to avoid long-term commitments. A reason given for this adaptation was that both the man and woman were very much involved with their career development and did not want to commit a greater amount of time to a relationship. The daters might also have relationships with out-of-town friends that would be activated only when that person came to town, or when they made plans to get together in another location. One woman said she had had a three-year dating relationship during her doctoral work. That relationship dissolved when she took an extended trip and found him involved with another woman when she returned.

One might expect that a dating relationship might be too tenuous for a woman to receive encouragement toward her career goals, but this was not the case. One woman said that all her male friends were quite supportive of her studies, and they often gave her encouraging words when she wondered whether it was all really worthwhile. Another woman commented that she felt most successful in her relationships when she was quite clear about what she wanted, and that included support for her goals. These women did not expect to derive all their support from the men they dated; perhaps because they did not, they were able to receive validation when they needed it most.

The daters with whom I spoke struck me as very egalitarian types. In describing components of their ideal relationships, they wanted partners who would be cooperative and certainly completely supportive of their decisions to pursue rather lofty career goals. One woman commented that she could not conceive of beginning a relationship with a man who did not accept unquestioningly her right to pursue her career. Another woman said her ideal mate would be a man with whom she could work, thus setting criteria including shared interests, equal educational attainment, and the ability to cooperate in reaching joint goals. These women set high standards both for themselves and their potential mates. They spoke with confidence about their ability to follow through with those expectations.

In considering future directions for their relationship lives, the daters seemed to either expect or hope that they would marry or form a supportive long-term relationship. They did not necessarily count a family as part of that equation, although they did not exclude that possibility. One woman told me (tongue in cheek, I believe) that she was planning soon to conduct interviews for a male "roommate." The daters fully intended to remain actively involved in their career development in conjunction with whatever new relationships might be formed. Each believed that no man is worthwhile who would want to restrict her free pursuit of an active career. For these women, relationships seemed to be a high priority, and they approached with confidence the challenge of forming relationships that would support and enhance their other life goals.

As a category, the daters seemed to have high self-esteem. Some were more confident than others, but all had developed comfortable strategies for finding their niches within that relationship game. One woman nicely illustrated this point when she told the following story. One evening she was involved in a romantic and intimate moment with a new man. As they stood on a balcony, he attempted to kiss her. Removing herself from his advance, she asked, "Just what is your goal here?" After some shocked deliberation, he answered that he thought he wanted to be her "knight in shining armor." She quickly responded, "I'm not sure that will work out, and besides, your horse would mess up my apartment."

THE ABSTAINER

In discussing with women doctoral students the different types of relationship styles, some stated that abstinence from intimate relationships was an option that did occur. The abstainers are women who have found that they could not effectively combine doctoral study and intimate relationships. Their chosen life-style seems to have been quite successful for them, and in at least some cases it was based on firm convictions.

Decisions to become abstainers may have been made consciously or unconsciously. A pattern seemed to be that these women found that their energies could not be expended in enough directions to include searching out and nurturing satisfying relationships. In at least two cases, women in this category terminated important intimate relationships early in their doctoral study. The period of study may then have constituted a hiatus for these women from a process that might bring rejections followed by more pain. Instead, they were able to devote their full attention to their career development, which provided greater personal rewards, at least for a time.

Since these women did not gain support from the traditional types of intimate relationships, they relied on other support groups. One woman indicated that her friendship network was almost exclusively female, and sometimes she even worried about whether she was too completely removed from the world of men. However, another woman said that most of the relationships she felt she could count on for support were with male friends whom she had known for some time. These women also directed significant amounts of attention to their family ties. In some cases this was a result of responsibilities to children or parents, while in others it was a continuation of a parent-child relationship that had grown highly supportive. These women were well aware of how their support systems functioned, and they indicated that they had made efforts to reinforce their effectiveness.

An abstainer volunteered some ideas that she had developed on ways to escape from the recurring frustrations of loneliness. She enjoyed reading novels, daydreaming, and some man-watching, but she devoted most of her time and caring to her close female friends. Another woman mentioned the sadness she felt in doing home maintenance tasks all alone. She did not complain about her lack of competence, but rather that it would be so much more enjoyable to share both the task and its completion with a partner. Although the abstainers expressed some unhappy feelings about their state, they were not overwhelmed by those feelings and seemed to deal with their situations very positively.

As abstainers spoke of their future plans for intimate relationships, there were wide variations. One woman indicated that she had every expectation of forming a special intimate relationship that she hoped would lead to permanency. She gave that fact some consideration when she chose her first job location. She wanted, if possible, to be in a city large enough to afford opportunities to meet a variety of people. In addition, she stated her confidence that she will be able to successfully merge the needs of her career development with the demands of that expected intimate relationship. She said simply, "It will fit." Taking a different position was a woman who said she could not really speculate on just what direction her involvement in intimate relationships might take. She indicated that she was very attuned to all the aspects of a particular context, and she would just have to wait and see how she felt about her fit into the new context she would enter after graduation. She allowed that she moved slowly and cautiously in such matters.

Contrary to what some readers might believe, the abstainers are not the most bookish of doctoral students who do not display sufficient social competence to establish intimate relationships. In those stereotyped respects, they could not be distinguished from the other categories. They did seem to express somewhat less confidence in their possibilities for establishing intimate relationships; that position, however, seems reasonable since they had placed themselves outside that whole game for the time being. Abstainers seemed particularly strongly committed to their career development and the challenges presented by doctoral study. They were willing to sacrifice some personal desires for what they saw as larger goals. They were proud of their accomplishments and took satisfaction from their considerable ability to cope with situations that some might decide to be intolerable. Their conviction must be admired.

THE SUSTAINERS

Sustainers are defined as those women who maintained one primary intimate relationship throughout the course of their doctoral study. The women interviewed for the purpose of developing these ideas were all married (although a sustainer could certainly be one who engaged in a nonmarried but committed and ongoing relationship). The combination of marriage and graduate study can be a very complicated one (see Chapter 9).

The sustainers probably represent more diverse methods of adapting relationships than any other group. Marriages ranged all the way from the traditional monogamous style with the female taking on most of the responsibility for family maintenance, to very cooperative relationships with nontraditional role definitions, to those couples in open marriages. The women with whom I spoke all were living with their mates during the doctoral program; however, it must be remembered that the stresses of graduate study can also sometimes include living apart from one's mate for significant periods of time. The threat of a separation recurs when women graduate and find that they must be mobile in order to maximize their possibilities for the best positions.

Among the sustainers, all their mates were at least passive supporters of their decisions to pursue doctoral study, and many were very active supporters. Support came most often in the form of approval and frequent encouragement when times were hard. Other valid support came from mates who shared household tasks, took over child-care responsibilities, and generally demanded less when they knew the stresses of study were great. A very competent and active woman joked about how her husband took pride in the decoration of their home, leaving her the decision of where one candlestick (it was a special one) would be placed. No one mentioned the husband who typed his wife's research papers, acted as editor, or spent hours quizzing her on materials for exams—behaviors that might be expected of a male student's wife. In general, most sustainers viewed their mates as quite supportive, although some mentioned ways in which they would have liked more affirmation. One woman said that she wished her husband would be more willing to discuss things with her from the practicalities of her day-to-day work, to broader "what-if" sorts of questions. Women appreciated what they got, but they also felt that in the same situation they would have been asked, and they would have given, more. This was particularly true of a woman whose husband was also in a doctoral program. She felt that much of the support and talking about problems went to him, leaving her to cope on her own or seek outside support.

Most of these women did develop networks for gaining support among their peers or other friends. Nevertheless, the intensity of marriage and family responsibilities may often leave these women somewhat on the outside of such networks. The woman with a husband waiting for dinner or children at home will not be able to stop with her friends for a drink or dinner after a late afternoon class. Likewise, she may have difficulty finding time to get together with other students outside class to work on a take-home exam or to do joint studying.

For a number of sustainers, the married relationship did not provide the only source of intimate relating. In some cases extra-marital associations became the glue that enabled the woman to tolerate and continue the marriage. However, for other women, those "flings" were only spice to an otherwise satisfying relationship. There were women who carried on secret relationships with other men for long periods of time. Other women engaged in affairs with the understanding and approval of their mates. One woman indicated that the openness of her marriage had been negotiated, but her husband asked that she not let him know of her liaisons, while she was interested in knowing about his! These descriptions are not meant to replicate any popular daytime dramas or to create ideas for new ones. However, they do illustrate that there are many possibilities for both women and men in designing intimate relationships that will be satisfying and sustaining.

What does the future hold for these couples who jointly negotiated the perils and stresses of doctoral study? Unfortunately, relationships are still vulnerable, particularly as the women seek positions and adjust to their new professional roles, which are quite different from those of subservient student. Many couples face the large problem of location. If a woman is offered an outstanding opportunity in another state, will her husband be agreeable and able to transfer his own profession to that location? One woman related that her husband has expressed a willingness to move once. Their plan is to move to a large metropolitan area that would provide multiple career opportunities for both, but the pressure is still on to find the job within that area. Other women have decided that their own professional development must remain second to the mate's job needs. Sometimes this is an economic necessity, while other times it is more related to the roles established for that particular pair. One apparently successful couple is made up of a woman university professor and her husband, who is pursuing a career in art. His work potentially could enable him to live in a number of locations convenient to her work needs. The women whose husbands can move with them are fortunate, but those moves do not preclude problems. One woman described the intense resentment her husband felt after moving to help further her career. He was able to move and retain his job, but since he had not decided on the new location, all its negative features seemed magnified many times over.

In addition to finding a mutually agreeable location, the couple still has the problem of dealing with the day-to-day sharing of maintaining a relationship and the space its partners occupy. Who will watch the home front when the new doctor takes off to attend several conferences, making presentations and reaping the rewards of all her hard work? Which partner deals with delivery and repair people who say they will arrive any time between eight and six? Some women are glad that their husbands also travel, as it leaves them large blocks of time to attack papers, write, or just have some privacy. Others have to work hard to carve out their own space and time at home.

Sustainers receive rewards from their stable and nurturing relationships; they do not, however, escape without adversity. In fact, some of their problems can be very divisive and soluble only with perseverance and creativity.

INTIMATE RELATIONSHIPS WITH PROFESSORS

Intimacy between physician and patient has been discussed more frequently as the medical profession faces the realities of its members' shortcomings. Intimate relationships between women doctoral students and professors are also a reality, but not an easy one to describe. Both the American Medical Association and the American Psychological Association have warned their members against this type of intimacy, and discussed the fact that it is both unethical and detrimental to the treatment process. How different is the professor-to-student relationship?

Many women come to graduate study with an idea that their professors are the ultimate in knowledge and understanding. If they are approached with the proposal of developing an intimate relationship, they may be more susceptible to that suggestion than they might be in other situations. Academic life fosters many professor-student marriages, but the graduate student underground also speaks of a number of relationships that did not have positive supportive consequences for the women involved.

Women become involved in intimate relationships with their professors for a number of reasons. They are vulnerable and need intimate support from someone they perceive as understanding of their goals and ambitions. They have access to inside information that may truly be helpful to them in negotiating their way through a doctoral program. They wish to please the professor whom they see as an authority. They would like to share not only the excitement of intellectual achievement but also continue that excitement to physical intimacy. They may wish to increase their chances of success in doctoral study (the casting couch may exist in academic circles). They may have fantasies of living and working with one person, experiencing the ultimate bond of work and love. All these reasons are based on human characteristics, and persons in academic life seem equally expressive of such characteristics, in spite of their intellectual strivings.

What happens to women who begin intimate relationships with professors based on some of that reasoning? There may be positive consequences, but there are some very negative outcomes as well. One woman found that the professor with whom she had established an intimate relationship became very testy and downgraded her work when they were placed in a supposedly cooperative working situation. Other women have found their own marriages or other relationships permanently disrupted because they have established intimate relationships with professors. Women also may be forced to lead their lives on several strata, being unable to share their whole experience with anyone because they must keep relationships with professors secret. For some women such clandestine intimacy remains to seem worthwhile, but others have said, "If I had only known! Never!"

What are the future expectations of a woman doctoral student who develops a relationship with a professor? Will she attempt to stay at the same university after graduation, existing on whatever positions her contacts can provide her? Perhaps she will move away to another position, leaving that relationship behind as a pleasant interlude that may remain supportive professionally if not personally. Such a move may also mean a wrenching experience. Will she be the woman whose confidence is destroyed after the professor-student relationship fails? Each woman must make her own choices. Several of the women interviewed said that they had elected to conscientiously avoid any appearance of intimacy with professors. They related strategies they had developed to keep relationships on a strictly professional level, including modesty of dress and ignoring any comment or suggestion that could be construed as sexual in nature.

The questions raised about intimacy between professors and students are sensitive. It is hoped that women doctoral students will consider some of these questions before they are faced with decisions. Certainly a cautionary message is in order.

SUMMARY

The women who chose to be makers and breakers of relationships, daters, abstainers, and sustainers all have star quality. They have learned to juggle their intimacy needs with the demands of career development. Perhaps it could be said that all women who choose to commit themselves to work outside their homes would experience similar styles of coping with that balance. The woman doctoral student is a special case in that she has chosen to set herself apart by gaining the highest level of educational achievement available in our society. The women represented within this chapter showed imaginative and often courageous ways of dealing with intimate relationships while pursuing the intellectual and career goals. They and I hope that the composite experiences presented will be helpful to other women as they sort their priorities and make their own decisions.

REFERENCES

Erikson, Erik H. Childhood and Society (rev. ed.). New York: Norton, 1963.

French, Marilyn. The Women's Room. New York: Summit Books, 1977.

_____. The Bleeding Heart. New York: Summit Books, 1980.

Gilligan, Carol. Woman's Place in Man's Life Cycle, Harvard Educational Review, 1979, 49, 431-446.

Katz, Joseph, and Hartnett, Rodney, eds. Scholars in the Making: The Development of Graduate and Professional Students. Cambridge, Mass.: Ballinger, 1976.

9

THE IMPOSSIBLE DREAM:
THE PH.D., MARRIAGE, AND
FAMILY

Linda S. Levstik

I do not know how many times during the last few years
someone has said to me, "Frankly, I don't know how you
do it. I could never manage to juggle graduate school, a
marriage, and children." Admittedly, there are easier
things to do with one's life, and had I to do it over again,
I might rearrange things a bit. But when I chose to begin my doctoral studies I had been married nine years,
our oldest child was five, and the youngest was just short
of a year old. I hadn't the faintest idea of what I was
getting myself into. I do not know if this chapter counts
as forearming, but I have tried to make it at least a
forewarning.

More and more women are moving into graduate school, pursuing the doctoral degree while coping with marriage and motherhood. Although the experience changes women and their families
and alters the nature of the graduate program, there is little institutional recognition of this phenomenon. Women are told often
enough that the divorce rate among graduate students is high, that
"of course" a woman's career options will be limited by her lack of
mobility, and that some faculty members will be hostile to admitting
a woman with children, especially if those children are young.
Graduate teaching and research assignments are handed out just
short of the start of each quarter, leaving scant lead time to arrange family schedules, and essential courses are invariably offered at impossibly inconvenient times. Finally, at graduation,
after the woman and her family have struggled diligently and creatively (one hopes) not just to survive, but to prevail, there is

recognition. Some official will smile benevolently on the assemblage and ask for applause for those family members the institution has hitherto failed to recognize. Congratulations. In spite of it all, you came through. You chose to attempt the impossible dream: pursuit of a Ph.D. and the maintenance of marriage and family.

Whether a woman ends the doctoral program with a strengthened family or a loosely affiliated assortment of people is determined, in large measure, by how creative and flexible each member of the family is. It is not easy. No matter what one thinks at the beginning, a Ph.D. will cost in ways not anticipated.

A FAMILY COMMITMENT

There are two kinds of families that find themselves facing a doctoral program. The first is the family in which husband and wife knew and agreed upon career goals for both partners. Part of the premarital commitment included graduate school for the wife. Whether this couple chooses to combine graduate school and young children or wait until the children are older, it is an established fact that the woman will pursue a degree and, therefore, a career. The fact that they also chose to have children may be a difficulty, but it is not a totally unexpected one.

The second type of family did not start out with such clear-cut goals. Perhaps a dual career was a precondition of marriage; perhaps not. At any rate, this couple finds itself having children. The wife may work. She may take time off to be at home with the children. At some point the woman's goals change. Whatever the precipitating factors, she finds herself moving in new directions— directions that require doctoral work. She has, in a sense, violated the expectations of her family (and herself). This need not be traumatic, but it does mean that she is at an initial disadvantage. She and her family may have considerably more adjustment to make than will the family for whom this is an anticipated turn of events.

In either case, the doctoral program must be a family commitment. The commencement speaker who applauded graduates' families knew that. What he most likely did not know was that the commitment necessitated by a woman's entry into the program is qualitatively different than that required for a man. The system supports men in pursuit of academic achievement. They are understood and forgiven much. Academic institutions assume, contrary to mounting evidence, that the man will be single or supported by a wife who can manage home and family on her own. The assumption is that male graduate students are unencumbered by multiple roles.

Women suffer for these assumptions. In spite of changes in the work and status of women, they are still expected, by themselves as well as society, to play the traditional roles of companion, housekeeper, mother, and hostess. A woman must, therefore, plan with her family to counteract the pervasive expectation that she will manage traditional roles while adding the roles of graduate student and often of teaching associate. Unfortunately, most women face this task with few role models and no guarantee that their planning will meet with success.

What planning can do is provide grounds for negotiation and establish the woman's graduate work as a family commitment. The alternative is unattractive. Without such a commitment, a woman is likely to find herself with a finite amount of time and an infinite amount of work. If this goes on too long, she may also work herself into physical and emotional exhaustion. Planning, then, is essential. Deciding what to plan for is equally important. Research dealing with dual-career marriages provides some insight into potential problem areas (Luring and Otto, 1976; Rice, 1979), but the order in which I have chosen to deal with them is based on personal experience. It may well be that childrearing is more crucial than housekeeping, but it is sometimes true that trivialities bury human beings.

POTENTIAL PROBLEM AREAS

Housework

Axiom 1: A scrupulously neat home and a doctoral program are mutually incompatible.

Axiom 2: To save time and energy one must spend money.

Women really cannot do it all. Do-it-yourself is a lovely, romantic notion bearing little or no relationship to the woman doctoral student. Survival demands that you learn to hoard time and energy, spending it only where it is most beneficial. This means that husbands share in significant ways. It means agreeing as a family that household chores will be shared, that some expectations will be lowered, others raised. It means learning to live with the fact that there are more books than clean socks in the house—even in the laundry room. This sounds simple enough until the issue of standards for work accomplished is raised. Some women find it extremely difficult to be satisfied with the rest of the family's standards. These women find themselves expending precious time and energy redoing what someone else has "finished." Rather than solving problems, this approach increases stress all around (see Chapter 6). The woman is furious and resentful; family members are not encouraged in their efforts. Everyone feels abused. One graduate student caught in this bind decided not to redo anything in preparation for her in-laws' visits. Everyone survived with the added bonus that her mother-in-law has taken to bringing extra food along on all visits. The graduate student decided to view this as a service rather than implied criticism; the children see it as a god-send in the light of grandmother's culinary skills.

For those with the financial resources, hiring housekeeping help is a wonderful investment. Even if it is just someone to come in and straighten up the place, make the beds and disappear, the psychic lift is worth the financial loss. Unfortunately, few graduate students can afford such a lift. Most must learn to live with a lot of mess, waiting for quarter break to dig out. A standard game among married student friends was a form of oneupmanship in which we traded disaster stories.

> "Some kid slammed into my car last night."
> "Oh, how awful!"
> "Yeah, especially since he knocked it backwards into my husband's car."
> "That's good, but listen to what happened to our basement. . . ."

The declared winner was the woman whose kitchen light fix-ture began leaking water one night—and it wasn't even raining; then the ceiling began sagging. . . . Anyway, she was supposed to be getting ready for generals, and there was this conference presenta-tion due. . . .

Finances

Axiom 1: A Ph.D. is an expensive degree in direct proportion to the cost of photocopying.

Axiom 2: No matter what you may have thought, neither love nor children survive well in a garret.

Axiom 3: If you want marriage, children, and a Ph.D., it is best to be an heiress. Second best is to marry rich.

There must be a woman doctoral student somewhere who is independently wealthy. Though I have never met her, I am envious. On the other hand, one might miss the experience of living as a graduate teaching or research associate. The community this pro-vides is wonderful. The financial aid, while deeply appreciated, is no princely sum. No one should be under the illusion that an assistantship in any way constitutes a second income. This is especially true when a graduate student is faced with child-care expenses, typing and photocopying expenses, and a compulsion to develop a personal library. In some cases, the stipend serves to push a family into the lower end of the next tax bracket, thus dramatically increasing the cost of the doctorate. Some universities justify providing minimal financial aid by explaining that the privilege of attendance should be worth the sacrifice. They are correct in assuming that part of the sacrifice required by a doctoral program involves financial loss. Not only does the student lose money while earning the degree, it has also become more likely that this loss will not be recouped. Assistant professorships do not pay well. In my field, the entry-level positions for Ph. D. s pay approximately $5,000 less than I could have earned by remaining in my former position. Your family needs to know this. One woman came to graduate school with her husband's blessing. For four years he counted on the financial rewards he assumed came with a Ph. D. He was horrified to discover that her first position paid less than her old job. Her children tease about their mother's uncanny ability to work harder for less.

Poverty is not romantic. The financial hazards of graduate school can be frightening. To begin with, it is difficult to prepare for the expenses involved in general exams or the dissertation process because the student has limited funds. Expenses depend on so many variables, including the type of study done, the fluctuating cost of typing, and the number of revisions demanded by a committee (see Chapter 3). As graduation approaches there is the additional specter of unemployment and the cost of sending out resumes and transcripts.

Time

Axiom 1: There will never be enough time while you are a graduate student.

Axiom 2: Time and temper are inversely proportional; as the first decreases, the second increases.

Upon completing a physical shortly after graduation, my doctor congratulated me on having withstood most of the vicissitudes of graduate school. Normally, he said, the frayed edges showed quite early and he saw more and more of the harried student. I, it seemed, was remarkably unfrayed. So much for cheap analysis. My facade was intact, at least in public, and my finances had kept me out of the doctor's office more often than had fortitude.

What the doctor had observed over the years, however, should be a warning to prospective graduate students. A doctoral program takes a physical and emotional toll (see Chapter 6). People change during the course of the program, and the dimensions of that change are influenced by several factors, including demands on time, emotional and intellectual powers, and the kind of support base available. Graduate schedules are erratic, flowing with the course of the academic year, not with life outside the university. As a parent, the woman doctoral student is torn. Papers become due, and so does a school concert or someone's birthday. The convention is held over Thanksgiving when historically the family gathers at grandma's. The deadline for the dissertation rough draft looms, and one of the children has to be rushed to the emergency room for stitches. Neither the woman's time nor her mental faculties are entirely at her disposal. The paper may be important and that deadline crucial, but neither will receive full attention if there is a sick child or an angry husband in the next room. Even healthy and happy families are a drain on time and energy. No matter how much they are loved, there will be times when the woman will wish them all on the far side of the moon. Just one hour of uninterrupted thought! She sits, desperately trying to compose the words to express an idea. A phrase slowly surfaces. It is so close. . . .

> "Mind if I come in a minute?"
> "Mmmm."
> "By the way, Sue and Tom thought they might drop by."
> "Aaah."
> "Are you listening?"

Unfortunately, she is listening. That perfect phrase has sunk beneath the waves of talk. She may be close to fury. Or tears.

Even where uninterrupted study time is arranged (no one is generous enough with that), if the family is within earshot, concentration lags.

> "Shh, damn it. Mommy's working."
> "But you can't braid my hair. That's not the way. . . ."
> "Hey, dad, where's mom? I want to show her something."
> "She's working!!!"

She, of course, is no longer working. Mom is gritting her teeth and considering soundproofing the office. Why do all these arguments occur just outside the office door? Perhaps mothers exude some magnetic force that draws the family to them. Perhaps it is a subconscious impulse to advertise their feelings of neglect. There will be a strong urge to tell them all to go away. Follow that urge. Arrange with the family for study time. If study must be done at home, agree to husband and children staying far enough away to allow for concentration. This can be a wonderful opportunity for fathers to do things with the children. Go hiking, go bowling, go swimming—but go! Do not stand around wondering why mom is close to tears when it is only the middle of the quarter. This is normal. If left alone, she will make it to the end of the quarter.

Because of academic pressure it is easier to arrange study time than to provide for time together, both as a couple and as a family. Neglecting time together can be disastrous. A doctoral program is going to be a strain—a three-year strain, on average. If a family is to survive there has to be time spent together. The house can wait; families cannot. This need can be an opportunity and an advantage. Women who devote themselves, body and soul, to the pursuit of a Ph.D. tend to burn out. They suffer physically, emotionally, and probably intellectually. Time spent away from academe can be healthy. Walking, playing, laughing—especially laughing—can restore balance. Get up and move around. Exercise. Talk about something other than school.

We hear so often about quality time being more important than quantity, but a relationship, whether with husband, child, or friend, needs both to flourish. Plan for quality time, of course, but plan, too, for just being there: time when the children know you are around if they need you. My daughter would go off to play while I worked on something in the office. The door was left open as a sign that I could be disturbed. She would come in every once in a while just to say hello. Sometimes she would bring me a bouquet of dandelions or clover, sometimes just a kiss before she ran off to play. My work got done; her need was also satisfied. Sometimes one of the children would call me out for a walk around the block. Ten minutes or so were all they wanted. My husband and I found the same thing helpful for us. His writing often consumes evening time as does my work. We often declare a break midway through the evening and go for a walk. The fresh air is invigorating, and the talk is good for us both. We reestablish contact and caring, and go back to work refreshed. That arrangement did not happen at first. It grew from a commitment to each other and the premise that isolated quality times were not enough. We needed more consistent time together. Otherwise, we discovered, neither of us could provide the kind of caring support the other needed, nor could we feel good about the time alone each of us required.

THE RENAISSANCE WOMAN

No matter how carefully preplanning is done, graduate school is still a surprise, as are the stresses that take their toll on the married woman student. Though there is probably no way to free oneself entirely of stress, it may sometimes be possible to draw advantage from adversity. One such area has to do with friendship patterns.

There is little if any institutional recognition of the needs of women graduate students who are married and involved in rearing children. As a result, they need graduate student friends, especially those who are also married and rearing children. They need them as a source of information—"Do I really need to form my committee this quarter?"—as a source of solace—"It is not you, he always edits like that"—and as a sounding board. This last is especially important in providing support for a difficult life-style. Graduate student friends can listen and share their own experiences (see Chapter 7). They know and sympathize with the problems of their colleagues. They can also see the humor in it all. One day, for instance, I observed my three-year-old playing with her dolls. She had decided to move on to something else, so she carefully laid each doll in the carriage, kissed them gently on the forehead, and said, "Be good, now. Mommy has to go to class." A neighbor to whom I related this incident shook her head and sighed. My graduate school friends laughed and shared similar tales. In the same fashion, colleagues nodded in recognition when my daughter explained that "Mommy finished the damn dissertation."

Perhaps, too, only another doctoral student could understand the woman who took her exams in her ninth month of pregnancy. Sitting was uncomfortable, so for three days, four hours each, she stood at a lectern, writing. The only problem, she said, was that one leg kept cramping up and interrupting her train of thought.

This shared context draws women graduate students together. It may also exclude outsiders—including husbands. Sometimes the result is a breakdown in "outside" relationships: "How could he possibly understand what I am going through?" Sometimes the result is to change marital assumptions. Both partners become more independent, while allowing their diversity of experience to enrich the marital relationship.

Graduate students also aid you in dealing with the pervasive male model of graduate education (see Chapter 5). Most graduate programs assume that their students come relatively unfettered. The student's time belongs to the graduate institution, and, like male faculty members, graduate students come either single or with wives who will take care of "real life" for the duration. When a married woman with children (especially young children) appears in this milieu there is consternation. A faculty member might suggest the woman student wait until the children are older. One woman faculty member has refused to accept advisees with preschool children. Another invariably recites the divorce statistics. The most unnerving aspect of all this is the underlying assumptions about women's career options and, ultimately, their seriousness in pursuing a Ph.D. The married woman must struggle against the notion that she will not be free to take the "good" positions, and therefore is not worth the investment of the adviser's time. Since she must stay, the reasoning goes, where her husband is, she cannot be terribly serious about all this. Because so few graduate institutions see a Ph.D. as leading anywhere but to teaching and research in another graduate institution, they perceive limited options for married women. As a result, such women are often left with little career guidance and no one who can effectively aid in the job search (see Chapter 11).

Misunderstanding is not limited to the university. The married graduate student also lives in a community. She has neighbors, maybe a house, and perhaps a sandbox and swing set in the backyard. Particularly if she has children, she must cultivate a friendly eccentricity or move into graduate housing. Children need neighborhood friends; the family does not need hostile neighbors. It helps, therefore, to be friendly.

My own neighborhood is small with an interesting mix of old, middle-aged, and young. Folks sit on front porches gossiping or just watching everyone else. They are not nosey so much as curious; thus the summer that I began typing the dissertation was a neighborhood event. For months I lived in the tiny second floor office, writing and typing. As the dissertation grew, I hung chapter outlines from the curtains where they flapped through summer days and nights. I often typed into the early morning hours. For days I only came out to cool off. Finally, one of the neighbors asked if I typed for a living. When I explained what I was doing she stared and said, "Oh, I didn't know you did that sort of thing."

Periodically I have spasms of normality during which I attempt to convince myself and the rest of the world that in spite of doing "that sort of thing" I am just an ordinary wife and mother. Somehow this seems to be translated into attending Tupperware parties. I invariably hate these gatherings and go home determined to find a better way of relating with neighbors. Evenings on someone's front porch are much better. People joke about my bizarre schedule and tease my husband about being neglected, but there is good-humored acceptance. Other married students report similar experiences. Neighbors sent food in for one husband while his wife worked on her dissertation. Another woman took the neighborhood kids to the university art program, studied while the children worked, came home and traded with another neighbor who shepherded the youngsters to the pool. Single graduate students often ask how anyone can manage to get anything done this way, and it is not easy. One mother of two reports that her adviser invariably called at four in the afternoon—right in the middle of the afterschool chaos. There were generally five children running through the house, and as anyone with children knows, the din increases as soon as a phone rings. The adviser commented that it sounded like D-Day.

"Only five kids," she responded.
There was a pause. "Five?!" her adviser cried.
"You have five children?"

Though she explained that only two were hers, the incident unnerved her adviser. He had never had to contend with such role switching. When he needed to make a phone call, his wife whisked children out of the way. If he chose to take or teach a four o'clock class, his wife was home to supervise the children. There was never any question of his rearranging his plans. The same professor later told his student that, had she been single and childless, she could have gone to the top of her field. She had yet to complete her degree, and her adviser spoke of her career in the past tense. Unable to handle diversity himself, he was convinced that she could not manage, either.

This is not an uncommon idea. An adviser might be forgiven, a bit, as he does not know the woman as well as he might. It is unnerving, however, when those who should know her best are equally doubtful. Parents, if not in-laws, should be supportive, but often are not. If not, they are best kept far, far away. These people are most effective in creating guilt and tension. Partly because their daughter's choice appears to be a criticism of their lives, mothers and mothers-in-law may begin a recurrent commentary on obligations to husband, children, and health. A fortunate few are gifted with relatives who support their graduate efforts. The rest hear about how awful the child-care arrangements are, how the house is collapsing, how they have not written or called, and, finally: "You know you don't react well to stress, dear. Why don't you take some time off and relax?"

In the face of this barrage, one can choose several alternatives: let it slide over without sinking in, take it to heart and make yourself miserable, or declare a moratorium on all such discussions. The scene may be painful, but for some it is necessary to redeclare their independence: "If we're going to talk, mom, we have to find something else to talk about." Having had mixed success in explaining myself, I have opted for silence. Others have found their parents become resigned and then, finally, excited and proud. Some even report a new, invigorating relationship, especially with their mothers. In the end the woman graduate student must be able to minimize the toll complex family relationships can take. She must allocate her energy carefully, be an adept at juggling a number of relationships and responsibilities, maintain a sense of humor, and be prepared for the unexpected. The graduate student, wife, and mother does the best she can and then learns to say, "I can afford no more. The rest is for me."

WHAT DO I DO NOW?

The dissertation is underway, graduation is a real possibility, a not some far-off, future possibility. The hard part is almost over, right? Wrong. A colleague warned me that the dissertation would look easy compared to the next step and I laughed. That was impossible, I said, from beneath a pile of books, chapter outlines, and note cards. But she was correct. The next step is much worse. Whatever questions about mobility, career opportunities, and future plans have been held in abeyance while the degree was completed now come to the fore. Where can a married woman with children find a position that meets the requirements of her own career goals, her husband's career goals, and her children's needs? (See Chapter 11.) It is likely that her husband is employed in the area where she has gone to school. It is equally unlikely that the university will hire its own graduates. Does the woman decide to relocate? Find a local position? Commute long distances?

There are no easy answers when couples contemplate dual careers. The choices can be made even more difficult if salaries are not conducive to easy moves or the expense of commuting. Children also complicate the decision. Will a new location have decent schools for the school-aged? Child care for preschoolers? If there are any special problems—medical problems, learning disabilities, handicaps—will a new location have support services?

The graduate institution is not likely to be very helpful at this juncture. Placing students in prestigious positions reflects well on the university. A woman looking into nonacademic employment may find that her adviser knows nothing of the world outside academe and is scornful of such positions. This means that career counseling is minimal, and once more the aspiring doctor finds herself left to her own devices. Eventually women may change the perceptions about career opportunities prevalent at graduate institutions. That does not seem to be happening at the moment, however. The emphasis is still on traditional career plans in spite of changing needs in academe, in the economy, and within the graduate population. At present, women should count on having to counsel themselves.

CAN IT WORK?

In spite of everything, can it work? It may be too soon to tell. Had I to do it over again, there is little doubt that I would make the same decision. I do not know whether it will be possible to manage the rest of a dual career. A sociology professor once told me that I could not have it all. She warned me, out of her own experience, that combining marriage, children, and an academic career was an impossibility. She chose to jettison her marriage, yet I quail at the thought of single parenthood and a career. If one human being can manage all that that entails, perhaps there is hope where there is an extra pair of hands.

REFERENCES

Luring, Rosalind K., and Herbert A. Otto. New Life Options. New York: McGraw-Hill, 1976.

Rice, David G. Dual-Career Marriage. New York: The Free Press, 1979.

10

GRANDMA!
WHAT BIG PLANS YOU'VE GOT!:
THE OLDER WOMAN'S PH.D.
EXPERIENCE

Mary Cay Wells

Although completing a Ph.D. in my fifties was not
especially unique, it clearly clinched my label as a
"mature" student. My experiences may or may not be
like those of other older women who have chosen the
doctoral route in middle age. I share my story for
what it was to me—a privileged adventure.

Even though, as a 22-year-old bride of two days, I registered
along with my husband for courses in a master's program, I fully
expected that my Haviland china, my sterling silver, and I would all
find fulfillment helping John do whatever he was destined for.

Twenty-eight (light) years later, fulfillment had mercifully
come in other guises: raising three children to productive adulthood,
keeping a marriage partnership viable for more than a quarter of a
century, and for me, an absorbing teaching career begun in my late
thirties.

I resonate with symbolism. That summer of 1976 was ripe
with it. We were rocking our first grandchild. We were still serving party-mix nuts from the wedding reception for our second
daughter. We were writing the last tuition checks for the last year
of college for our third and last child. My mother, our sole surviving parent, was slowly recovering from a serious illness.

These indications of middle age were the familiar part of the
picture. Besides these, I had been granted a year's leave of absence from teaching. A graduate teaching associateship, to my
initial astonishment, was waiting for me at the university. My
social and community obligations were pared to the bone. All signs
pointed to a 90-degree bend in the road. I, a 50-year-old grandmother, was about to start a doctoral program.

It was time. The peripheral issues had been raised and discussed many times by John and me. Could we afford to forfeit three years of my earning power? We could. Should we give up three or even many more years of credit in my retirement plan? We'd risk it. Could I make it academically? Good grades in several trial-run courses seemed to indicate so. Would my projected age at graduation—53—affect my chances for being hired in a different capacity? We would risk that, too.

Finally, it came down to two basic questions. First, did we have the adaptiveness as a couple to deal with one Ph.D. between us—held by the woman? We eventually decided we did. The big question remained. Only I could answer it. Was I truly Ph.D. quality?

The response to that question was at least four years forming. It started with some turns in my professional life: several challenges were successfully met; a rare opportunity put me in the company of stimulating people and ideas for three years on a special school project. Next, I began to be aware that I was seeking out persons with broader perspectives to talk with, learn from, and be friends with. I noticed that I often thought and operated as they did. Finally, at different times, three or four mentors (both male and female) nudged me toward dealing openly with the possibility of studying for a doctorate. When all the redundant (but necessary) processing wound down, I was comfortable saying, "Yes, that's where I'm headed, and I'm ready to begin."

Clearly, my view of myself had changed since my honeymoon.

SETTLING IN

The all-enveloping, phenomenal, emotional, ever-to-be-remembered experience of earning a Ph.D. began that fall. A three-day orientation for our teaching associate (T.A.) group of ten gave a fleeting overview of our teaching responsibilities. The seminars were led by second- and third-year doctoral students. I was impressed by their capabilities and knowledge and looked up to them—I a matron of 50 with 12 years' public school experience, to their average age of perhaps 30. Age, sex, competence, and station in life were already scrambled in this context.

As the pace of the beginning of the university year picked up, I had an agreeable sense of anonymity. Few knew or cared about who I "had been," how my husband earned his living—indeed, if I had a husband. I wondered briefly how many of my 50 years were noticeable. No one offered a clue. I was relieved. This was wonderfully here and now.

We T.A.s rated ancient desks distributed among the outer offices of several of the department's tenured professors. The established T.A.s warned us that the first week of school we women would be pestered with questions by other students who took us for secretaries. We were advised to head this off. We placed a male student at the desk closest to the door. We tacked a sign on the outer office door indicating where the main office and all the department secretaries were located. We sat inhospitably with our backs toward the door. And still the students approached us women, passed our signs, passed the fellows, and went around our turned backs to ask us about a professor's schedule or the location of the restrooms. Being taken for a secretary made some angry. In my strange state of perceived anonymity, I was less angry than annoyed at being continually interrupted as I tried to read my first assignments.

The first question people ask when they react to my returning to school as an older student is "Didn't you find it terribly hard to get back into the swing of studying again?"

I have to reply not really. I had been reading professional literature. Seeking out and assimilating new ideas were by now part of my life. What drove me wild as a new graduate student, however, was the impossibility of completing assigned work or inquiring into sufficient depth into some new topic. One could apply every spare moment and every last ounce of energy without achieving closure. I was very uneasy coming to class in this state of relative preparedness. In time, I took cues from several of my professors who well understood that one never truly and fully "knows," and I learned better to tolerate this ambiguity.

A significant facet of my settling-in period was a sorting of my life into two worlds: the graduate student's and the suburban woman's. Geographically, the two were 13 miles apart. Monday through Friday, including most evenings, belonged to me, the graduate student. The university was my turf. I absorbed the graduate school culture and spent my time with colleagues with like interests. The two evenings a week my husband worked in the city I felt free to stay at the university, make supper arrangements near the campus with friends, or work at the library if I did not have an evening class. The suburb seemed a world away during the week. It could not easily intrude on me, the graduate student, and I felt the protection of 13 miles of freeway five days of the week.

On the other hand I, the suburbanite, had to make do with Friday evenings, Saturdays, and Sundays. Stuffed into two-plus days were all household maintenance tasks, socializing with friends, church activities, and family get-togethers. As if these did not crowd the constricted two-and-a-half day weekends, I, the student, always needed hours for extra studying and appropriated time shamelessly from me, the lady of the house. Weekends were often so full that Sunday evening would find me wishing I had studied more. Still, I was torn by the knowledge that one day graduate life would be phased out, and I certainly did not want to find John and me bereft of friends and family when life returned to normal. Paradoxically, weekends were sometimes the focus of more personal tension than were the weekdays with their own rigors. The push and pull of both kinds of demands generated my personal definition of ambivalence: settling down to write a term paper when one suddenly hears a grandchild's voice at the front door. At that point, the definition ceases to hold, and the irresistible qualities of that sound transcend whatever it is I thought I had to do.

The settling-in period lasted the first quarter. As a group of us celebrated with hamburgers the day winter vacation began, I recall the shared sense of achievement as we told each other we had lasted through one term. We had survived intact. We were bona-fide Ph.D. students.

THE ONGOING EXPERIENCE

I easily subscribed to life as a graduate student. Interesting and exciting people come to mind first. Among new friends I counted persons from Indian, Jewish, Afro-American, Greek, Nigerian, Iranian, and Australian cultures. They ceased to seem different, even in native garb.

We had easy access to the "greats" whose professional lives often touch a university. A prized memory is that of hearing the indomitable Margaret Mead speak to an overflowing auditorium of students, just six months before her death. It occurred to me that not many 52-year-old gray-haired ladies like myself were finding happiness perched on a step in a crowded aisle for an hour and a half, but I was not about to suggest a trade with anyone. The great lady autographed my copy of <u>Blackberry Winter</u>. I treasure it. Ralph Tyler, Laurence Cremin, Maxine Greene, Art Combs, and others came our way. We graduate students had only to make room in our schedules and we could hear or speak with these persons.

Many of our professors were of very high caliber also. I occasionally jogged my consciousness—not about their exceptional qualities, because those were evident, but that I was privileged to know them on a personal, daily basis.

The friendships and relationships with my colleagues were and are the essence of the Ph.D. experience for me (see Chapter 7). The acknowledgments page of my dissertation recognizes "fellow

graduate students whose companionship has immeasurably invigo-
rated, diversified, and augmented the experiences of these three
years." This appreciation is real. Among these friends are experts on group process, Carl Jung, the day-care movement,
anthropological research methods, middle school curriculum,
Perry's important work in the stages of intellectual and ethical development of college students, environmental psychology, and
teaching teachers to help students be creative. They were willing
to share what they were learning and integrating, and just as freely
became sounding boards for someone else who needed to talk to
hear herself think.

Friendships spilled over from academic contacts and touched
me socially. John and I were graciously included in potlucks,
picnics, and other get-togethers. John also came to enjoy the
diversity and substance of these folks and gained several good
friends from within this group.

If friendships were the essence of the Ph.D. experience,
food—communally consumed—was its fuel. The mention of deep-
dish pizza, Greek gyros and baklavas, or vegetarian menus, all
new to me initially, elicits instant salivation. A still-warm toasted
bagel brought fresh from the Levy breakfast table one dark, sub-
zero morning, still stands at the top of remembered eating pleasures.

While age categories remained obscure and of little real im-
port, there was some mutual curiosity across generational lines.
The university is essentially a childless culture. Of the graduate
students I knew, more were single than were married, and of the
latter, only a few had children. My friends were very attentive to
details about the young children in my life, my grandchildren. They
asked me about their development, their upbringing, and their
parents' attitudes. They followed both my daughters' pregnancies
and Lamaze classes with high interest. One friend asked me to
join her for lunch one day to describe day-to-day minutiae about
schedules, feeding, and caring for babies.

Although these young professionals were not preoccupied with
their relationships with their parents, they spoke of them upon
occasion. I listened to conversations about their mothers or fathers,
but my colleagues seemed not to associate me with the next-older
generation. It apparently did not often occur to them that I, as a
parent of grown children, might have a point of view similar to that
of their parents.

A still-vivid conversation occurred one noon as several students brown-bagged it in the office. Triggered by a now-forgotten
comment, I mentioned that each of our grown children has his or
her key to our house, while we do not have keys to theirs. The
group lunching and chatting immediately confirmed this to be true

for them as well. Many, upon reflection, decided this was unilateral. One couple "turned in" their parents' house key the following weekend.

Their various curiosities could not equal mine about their single life-styles. Having moved from my father's home to one with my husband, I had never had my own apartment, lived alone, or worked to support just myself. I was inordinately inquisitive about how it is to live by oneself, buy one's own car, cook for just one person, travel alone, and be responsible for just oneself. I had fleeting moments, especially on those jam-packed weekends, when the single life looked mighty inviting. My perspective always returned quickly, however, when I noted the drawbacks and recalled my advantages. These young people had turned their backs on financial security for the duration of their Ph. D. programs and were coping uncomplainingly with often woefully inadequate funds for ordinary and simple amenities. I admired them greatly for their abilities to manage and to gripe so infrequently. Certainly, having a husband as financial backup (to say nothing of other kinds of support) was one of the most obvious advantages of earning a Ph. D. as an older woman.

Having been a Ph. D. student years before, my husband had some sense of my experience. His experience, however, had not been an enjoyable time for him. He may have envied me the pleasures my program provided me, but harbored no wish whatsoever to exchange his A. B. D. (All But Dissertation) for his Ph. D. at this late date.

John assumed a quiet but extremely supportive behind-the-scenes role. Besides sharing cooking, shopping, and laundry chores, he adapted gamely to a less-than-neat house for days on end. He never complained about a curtailed social schedule. His attitude was one of advocacy for me and my goals. If it was a sharp evolution for me in ways of rethinking my role as a woman, it was even more drastic for him. We began to understand with fresh insight how the dynamics among all family members must inevitably shift when changes occur in even one person.

Serendipitously, perhaps, one turn of events handily tied up two loose threads: one, my inordinate time commitment away from home, and two, my modest success in my new undertaking. Soon after I began my program, John opened an after-hours private practice, something he had wanted to do for a long time. It proved to be a highly successful venture for him, both professionally and financially. On one hand, his time investment balanced mine: we each had an interest equally absorbing. On the other hand, his success in a business venture of his creation was a counterpart to my success at the university. John sees himself, as I do, as having personal security and maturity both in his willingness to be a champion for my goals then, and now as a partner with "Dr." Wells. We have been fortunate to have been able to adapt and grow as a couple in this joint venture.

PANICS, PLAINS, AND PEAKS

Others have described the checkpoints and hurdles necessarily encountered by all doctoral students who stick it out. The three years are an emotional binge: anxiety, affirmation, depression, euphoria, terror, and ecstasy. Most students have these feelings.

The first of the panics hit me in the middle of my first quarter. I suddenly realized that in four to six quarters I would be expected to take qualifying exams. They loomed immense and unmanageable. A friend and I were consumed by anxiety (see Chapter 3). One of those high-caliber professors took the time to calm us down and reassure us of the benign intent our faculty had regarding these exams. From then on, I was acutely interested in others' experiences, including not-so-helpful horror stories. I mentally prepared and rehearsed until it was my turn six quarters later. Panic hit several times as I began the long countdown.

Another kind of panic enveloped me for a few days after I had gathered my research data. It looked . . . so . . . so sparse! I could not believe ten weeks of data gathering had produced so little. I was so persuaded this was true that I nearly succeeded in convincing my adviser as well. Luckily, we both regained perspective, and I eventually found that what I had was not only sufficient, but was also a large quantity.

A third panic was short but intense. One of my audiotapes of precious primary data was inexplicably and totally blank when I sat down at the typewriter to transcribe it. A rescheduled interview with one of my subjects probably recaptured the essence of the data, but not before I spent a miserable 48 hours convinced of the failure of my study.

Plains, or lows, are different from panics. They flatten, immobilize, and sometimes open the door to anger. The first quarter I taught a regular section of university juniors, I struggled with zeroing in on their level. I learned by not-very-funny trial and error how much they differed from fifth graders and from classroom teachers. I was so sure I had botched the job that I graded their exams in a fit of depression, refusing to read their anonymous evaluations until I had finished. That was a vivid lesson to me in what a closed state of mind does: it keeps out both the undesirable and the desirable. The evaluations were very positive, and a permanent depressive state was handily averted.

I still bristle at the recollection of criticisms a professor leveled at a term paper into which I had poured myself. Even my basic assumptions were questioned. Unable to fight back, I simply cut off any significant interaction with him in the future. This was not a very straightforward approach, but it was all I could handle at the time.

A crowded summer class was the source of another low. By the end of each class I was ready to (and occasionally did) explode in anger and frustration at the professor's continually changing expectations and directions for the class.

Peaks? They are the mountaintops. They outnumber the panics and the plains combined. They are what make it all worthwhile. They are the best remembered.

The discovery of split-brain research and my integrating it into my thinking was an early high. The whole concept has layers of meaning for me that continue to reveal themselves. I wrote a term paper on this topic, on an intellectual high, and was affirmed by the professor clear into orbit.

A little paperback by Art Combs opened double doors to the theory that framed some of the knowings I had.

A course in educational anthropology opened me to ethnographic methods and qualitative analysis of data. When events like this suddenly let in fresh air and breezes, the highs feel one mile up.

My turn at general exams was the most wildly emotional, intense, introverted, affirming experience of my entire Ph.D. program. One thousand of Margaret Mead's native tribes could not have dreamed up such a rite of passage into Ph.D. candidacy: three half-days of writing absolutely all you know, followed in ten days by a two-hour oral exam by five professors. The sense of "well done" was impetus through to graduation one-and-a half years later. Unlike some, I did not experience the six-month, nonproductive hiatus afterward, but really felt lifted toward work on my research proposal and subsequent study.

Dissertation writing was a singular experience (see Chapter 4). I liken it to being in an altered state of consciousness day after day. It was a very agreeable condition of intense focus and preoccupation with the task, a shutting out of all else. I begrudged time out to eat and sleep because I would have to shift out of this productive state and lose temporary touch with where I was. Never again will I have the privilege of being that immersed in something for that extent of time, about two months. The euphoria as I finished was monumental. Even graduation itself, a wonderful high, did not compare with the realization that I really wrote a dissertation.

A number of traditions, mostly gustatory, sprang up around these landmark events. Considering the affect connected, it is no wonder we celebrated by eating. Women's lunches became a regular event every few weeks. Some of us who had survived a difficult class together kept in touch this way and introduced our friends to other women. Lunches during the three days of generals writing were regularly scheduled by friends of the writer. A shared bottle of wine was a custom after the final exam day. Weekday lunches could always be eaten informally in the company of friends brown-bagging also. A cake and posed pictures on certain steps at the front of the building became a year-end tradition for our T.A. staff. A very supportive ritual was the custom of notes, flowers, or cards for those taking comprehensives or defending dissertations, with close friends waiting outside during orals in order to congratulate first. Joint graduation parties drew common friends and afforded a final, exhilarating celebration before the Ph.D. experience became a memory.

LOOKING BACK

Being age 50 at the start of my program and 53 at graduation places me unequivocally in the older woman category, defined elsewhere as over 50. Standing on this experience and looking back, I sometimes feel astonished that it could have happened to me.

My adulthood has encompassed living on one income and sharing one car. I was advised kindly that I should pick a career, teaching, for instance, which was more fit for a woman than one that could be competitive with my husband's. Only yesterday, relatively speaking, I used my husband's credit cards and could not have been granted a bank loan, even though I had regular income. I have heard open criticism of mothers who worked. I have seen eyebrows raised at women who wanted careers, or ate lunch in public places with men other than their husbands, or made speeches in public, or expressed opinions on politics. Women in executive positions and those on equal professional footing with men were a novelty. It was difficult to find feminine role models. It still is.

I believe these factors and others help account for my difficult coming to grips with the decision to earn a Ph.D., the inordinate delay in my starting, and the lack of a sense of resentment in re-assuming the subservient schoolgirl, student role.

I had simply waited it out—for about 25 years. I waited until our children were grown and educated, until there was sufficient financial support, and until my husband and I could feel secure in a relationship that had visibly altered over the years and that might evolve even more. Biding my time, albeit subconsciously, was my way of dealing with the obstacles.

Earning a Ph.D. as an older woman has much to recommend it, however. It circumvented some financial problems, as well as stress related to responsibilities for dependent children. Menopause passed by unnoticed. I was granted a reprieve from playing a kazoo with the Golden Agers at the state fair. I needn't sign up yet for tours on the community senior citizens bus.

Perhaps I am a bridge between some women of my generation who have not yet risked rethinking their directions, and those younger women who have taken the big step early to allow for a lifetime of professional productivity.

I have no regrets. The doctoral experience as an older woman was my lifetime high.

11

THE JOB HUNT

Marion R. McNairy

With three chapters of a dissertation to finish, I was interviewed in May for an early childhood education position at Indiana University. I was extremely nervous before the interview. After all, IU is a Big Ten School and third in the nation in education. Why would they ever want me ? Just before I was to begin the schedule of interviews, I made a conscious decision based on the following: I am a human being; I am a competent professional person; I have had many rich and exciting experiences, including those restricted to females (giving birth and continued nurturance to three sons); I am proud of being a human being who is female, who is also an individual. And I genuinely care about other people. I decided to hold my head up and be ME in all the richness and complexity of personhood. I was hired that day.

All the time spent in study, all the personal and professional growth, all the highs and lows of graduate school culminate, toward the end of the Ph.D. program, in that activity known as the job hunt, or, more formally, seeking a professional position. At this time,

―――――――――

I am greatly indebted to Dr. Ann Shelly for her invaluable insights and practical hints on the process of the job search. Much of the information presented in this chapter is a summary of information given to me by Dr. Shelly in informal conversations.

we put ourselves on the line, saying: "This is who I am. This is what I can do. This is what I want to do." It is at this time that we are the most vulnerable, for our years of effort are to be judged by others. It is true that we have faced judgment before, but the judgment was clouded by the egos and needs of those who taught us or under whom we studied. Now, the judgment is objective, and we will be found acceptable or wanting.

Much of the stress connected with the activity of searching for a job results, to some degree, from the absence of personal control over decisions made by others concerning our life. Once we have presented ourselves to others, the process becomes one of waiting until a committee, an administrator, or an Affirmative Action officer has decided whether we are acceptable or wanting for a particular position at a particular time.

Since we have so little control over the decisions of others, the purpose of this chapter is to share ideas about those areas in which we do have control, that is, the processes involved in the search and the presentation of self throughout phases of the search. The chapter reflects the experiences of one who had previously decided to seek an academic position in an institution of higher education.

A NOTE ABOUT TIME

The job hunt begins approximately six to eight months prior to the beginning of the academic year. This may present some candidates with the first major problem: the conflict between the job search and finishing the dissertation. As each activity is severely demanding of both time and effort, it is better to try to finish the dissertation before the beginning of the job search. If that is not possible, one must recognize, and be prepared to accept and cope with, the fact that the intensity of the "altered state of consciousness" involved in dissertation writing (see Chapter 10) may be shattered, and one may become involved in a continual juggling act, with time replacing juggling pins.

The critical period for watching for notices of available positions is usually from January through March. Occasionally there may be a second wave of listings in late April and May. This is the result of late budget clearings for new positions or late resignations from already existing positions. Very few notices are listed at other times.

Once a job has been posted, there is usually a stated deadline for applications to be submitted. After that deadline, a period of anywhere from two to eight weeks (or more) may elapse before the candidate is notified of her or his status regarding the particular position.

If the candidate is requested to visit the university or college for an interview, another two to four weeks may pass before the final decision is made for that particular position. Rarely is the candidate asked on the spot to accept the position, but it has been known to happen.

These notes about time have been included to underscore the idea that the processes involved in the search for a position may be very time consuming. If patience is not already a virtue, it soon will become one.

WHERE TO LOOK

As one approaches the job hunt, the first bewilderment may concern the question, "Where do I begin to look?" There are six primary sources when looking for a position. Be sure to utilize all of them.

Read the Chronicle and pray! This advice, frequently given to prospective employees, contains the truth that the Chronicle of Higher Education is the first place to look. The Chronicle is a weekly newspaper that is published throughout the year. The annual subscription rate is, at the present time, $25. The entire middle section of the publication is devoted to posting of jobs in all academic areas. At the beginning of the classified section is an index to the postings. Be sure to look under all possible headings that may pertain to your field, including the heading of assistant professor. Headings are listed alphabetically, but there are also freestanding ads, so carefully check the entire classified section.

A second source for finding job listings is your university personnel placement office. Your university may have more than one office. In some large universities, education, for example, may have its own office. Be sure to check for all possible placement services your university may offer. Frequently, placement offices have weekly, biweekly, or monthly mailings that list positions sent to them from across the nation. A job hunter can be placed on placement office mailing lists for a nominal fee. It is also helpful to become acquainted with the placement officer, who then may contact you when a position that meets your needs comes into the office. This is a key person in the job hunting process.

Your department chairperson is the third primary source for job listings. Notices of vacant positions are frequently sent to the chairperson. However, you must maintain contact with that person, as she or he may not remember you when a job comes across the desk. Your chairperson may also learn of positions at conferences. Be sure to check with the chairperson upon her or his return from those conferences. The chairperson may post job listings on an office bulletin board. Check these frequently.

A fourth source for job listings consists of journals in your field. For example, the author's field is early childhood education, and journals from the fields of home economics as well as from early childhood education were checked.

Professional conferences are a fifth source of potential jobs. Many disciplines have an annual conference sponsored by their professional organization. Frequently, positions will be posted on a bulletin board. However, these conferences can even be more helpful by helping you meet potential employers in your field. If universities hold open houses at the conference, attend them. If your major adviser or chairperson is also attending the conference, have that person introduce you to others in your field. The purpose here is to make contacts that may be beneficial to you during your current job search or during a later search.

Another type of conference is one sponsored by an organization that cuts across fields. In the field of education, one such conference is the one sponsored by the American Association of Colleges for Teacher Education (AACTE), which is held annually in February. At this conference, three rooms are set up for placement purposes. In the candidates' room are found volumes of job listings, separated by fields within education. In the employers' room are found comparable volumes filled with vitae or resumes of prospective candidates. All candidates and prospective employers are issued a number. With the use of cards and a mailbox system, candidates and employers may contact each other to indicate interest in an interview. Interviews may be held either in the third room at the conference center or at a particular university's suite in a hotel. A word of warning: a woman should be careful about going into a male employer's hotel room by herself. Some men have been known to want more than an interview. If the person interviewing you does not have a suite, suggest meeting that person in the conference interview room.

A sixth source for potential jobs is comprised of graduate students and other faculty in your field. Even though you are, in a very real sense, in competition with other graduate students, you can be of help to each other. The author went through the job hunt with Sue Vartuli, the editor of this book. We found that even though we had similar backgrounds, each of us had strengths the other did not. But more important, we discussed our feelings about being in competition as well as alternatives in dealing with these feelings. Throughout the job hunt, we became even more supportive of each

other, listening to each other's fears, hurts, and joys. Each week
we would compare what each had found in the Chronicle or other
sources, and one often supplied information the other had missed.

In addition to other graduate students providing a support system and sources of information, faculty also can provide information and support. Frequently, faculty members in your field may
hear of positions before they are posted. Keep in touch with them,
as they can be most helpful.

These six primary sources provide alternatives for beginning
the search. Perhaps the most important factor is that one should
not limit oneself to only a few sources. Try them all!

PREPARATION OF SUPPORTING MATERIALS

In anticipation of the active job hunt, three types of supporting
materials should be prepared: a resume or vita, university personnel placement office credentials, and copies of publications or papers
in preparation or submitted for publication.

The resume is an important document because it provides an
"in-a-nutshell" view of who you are and what you have done. The
contents should include: your name, address, telephone number,
and social security number; your educational background, including
the names of institutions you have attended, the dates of attendance,
degree earned, major field of study, and title of thesis and dissertation; your professional background, including dates of employment,
name and address of employer, your title, and a brief description of
your primary responsibilities during the term of employment; consultant and workshop experiences, including dates, names of institutions you have served, content of workshops, and responsibilities
incurred as a consultant; professional and civic involvement, in
which you list all professional organizations to which you belong,
as well as religious and civic groups; publications, which should
include all papers that have been published, have been submitted
for publication, or are in progress toward publication; and references, which should include the names, titles, and addresses of
three to five persons who would be willing to support you if and when
contacted.

The appearance of your resume is extremely important. This
document represents you and should reflect your best qualities.
Since prospective employers have many resumes to read, yours
should be neat, arranged in an orderly fashion, and easy to read.
No one wants to wade through pages of information to find essential
data. The paper you use for printing or xeroxing your resume
should be white, ivory, buff, or light gray. A friend of the author's

commented that one resume she had received—printed on bright
pink paper—was certainly eye-catching, but also most offensive.

Approximately 25 copies of the resume should be printed or
xeroxed. You will probably be applying for between 10 and 20 positions, and each position will require a copy. You may also want
extra copies for distribution at conferences and workshops. It is
not economical, however, to have too many copies made, as some
of the information on the resume will be obsolete within six months
and changes will have to be made.

In addition to the resume, you should contact your university
or education personnel placement office for the forms needed to
compile your credentials. The placement office has forms that,
when completed by the candidate, are stapled together and can be
sent to prospective employers at the request of either the candidate
or the employer. The forms will ask for information about the following areas: educational background, including degrees attained,
courses, grades, and professors in major and minor fields; professional experiences; references, which include the names of at least
five persons who represent your doctoral program, your master's
degree program, professional experiences, and a general personal
reference; and letters of recommendation, generally from your committee chairperson, faculty in minor areas of study, your master's
degree adviser or chairperson, and a person with whom you have
worked in a professional situation. Also included in the credentials
packet may be a page entitled the candidate's page, which provides
the candidate an opportunity to express her or his professional
philosophy, goals, and research interests. Although some candidates feel it is unnecessary to complete this page, utilizing it does
allow the candidate to give a personal impression, which may be
helpful to prospective employers.

Like the resume, the placement credentials represent the
candidate. They should be carefully prepared and neatly typed. A
word of warning: among the forms to be filled out for the placement
office may be one requesting the candidate's sex, age, marital
status, and number of children. The candidate is not required to
provide this kind of information to any prospective employer in
either written or verbal form if the candidate does not wish to do so.

In addition to providing the forms for the credentials packet,
the personnel placement office may offer additional aid. Use it.
Members of the placement office can help you prepare your resume,
provide feedback on your letters of application, and give you an idea
of what to expect in an interview. They can be very helpful and supportive in a situation in which the candidate needs lots of both.

In addition to the resume and the credentials, a third type of
supportive material may be requested by a prospective employer.

This includes copies of articles written by the candidate that have been published or are in the process of being submitted for publication, as well as answers to questions submitted by the search committee. These questions may be somewhat similar to generals questions and are meant to be indicative of your philosophy, goals, or research interests. The candidate should be prepared for this kind of request by having developed several papers (in the case that the candidate has not been published) and by thinking of answers to potential questions. A major adviser and a departmental chairperson are good sources for the types of questions that may be asked.

The preparation of supporting materials—resume, placement credentials, and additional materials—should be done prior to the active job search. "Be prepared" is a useful motto not only for Boy Scouts. It's imperative for job hunters.

ANSWERING A JOB POSTING

Answering a job posting means letter writing. Each letter should contain information about you and your interest in the position. Many people say that your letter should be brief and that you should let your resume speak for you. However, other advice was offered to and accepted by this author, who, finding it to be quite successful, will pass it on.

The letter you send should consist of four paragraphs. In the first paragraph you should state that you are applying for a particular position and name the source and date of the advertisement you saw. Be sure to be specific about the position for which you are applying, as a school or department may be posting for more than one position. Mentioning the source and date of the advertisement helps the search committee determine the best use of advertising dollars. This paragraph should also include a general reason for your interest in the position. You might mention the reputation of the school or the potential for professional growth in a particular geographical region as a general reason for your interest.

The second paragraph should tell specifically why you think you are suited to the position. This indicates to the search committee that you have read and understand the job requirements, and it allows you to highlight your professional experiences that enable you to perform the duties involved in the position.

In the third paragraph you should indicate more general things about you that make you a good person to have around. Include a brief description of your research interests. Be sure to keep this section short.

In the final paragraph, describe what supporting material you have enclosed with the letter and any materials you are having sent to the search committee. You should enclose a copy of your resume and articles, if requested, with your letter. In addition, you should have a copy of your placement credentials and copies of both under-graduate and graduate transcripts sent to each search committee. This may be somewhat expensive, but it shows your prospective employer that you are organized, and it saves the search committee chairperson from having to request these materials. You might end your letter by indicating that you are willing to send additional information as needed and hope to have the opportunity to visit the campus.

The appearance of your letter is as important as the appearance of your resume. Use white, ivory, buff, or dove gray paper. If you use a letterhead, have paper printed with your home address and telephone number. It is considered tacky to use your university letterhead. It is also a good idea to have the paper match the paper used for your resume. Make sure there are no typing errors, strike-overs, cross-outs, or spelling or grammatical errors. This letter must look professional.

It is very helpful to keep a file of jobs for which you have applied. Ads can be clipped out and taped to a piece of paper. The source and date of the ad can be noted on the paper, as well as the date that you sent the cover letter. You can also note the date on which you requested transcripts and credentials to be sent to the search committee. Attach a carbon copy or a xeroxed copy of your cover letter to the paper, and then add any additional information or letters sent to you by the search committee.

Once you have begun to apply for positions, you get a sense of "at least I'm doing something constructive." But the hardest part is still ahead.

WAITING FOR THE RESPONSE

Waiting to hear from the search committee is, at best, un-bearable. At worst—and there are those times—it is sheer hell. The anxiety, the extreme strain, the questioning of one's own worth puts general exams and dissertation way down on the list of difficult times. However, some information about timing may alleviate a little of that anxiety.

An ad is usually placed in the Chronicle for two or more weeks. The ad will state a closing date for the search, which is generally a month from the first posting. After the closing date, the search committee reads all the resumes and supporting materials and nar-rows down the possibilities to about ten people. They then reread the materials and narrow down the candidates to the top three or five. This process can last anywhere from two weeks to three months.

Two possible alternatives end the waiting period. The first, and hardest to live with, is the rejection letter. The first rejection letter is probably the most depressing, but each continues to hurt. It can be helpful to have a friend with you when you read these letters, or at least be able to use one or all of your support systems to weather these times. The second alternative is the telephone call asking you for an interview. This is a time of elation that also should be shared with your support system.

A question frequently arises concerning phone calls during the waiting time—who makes them and what should be said. You have the right to call a search committee chairperson if you have been asked for an interview at a different institution but are interested in the first. When you make this call, it is considered bad form to ask, "Do I have a chance for this job?" Rather, you can ask, "When do you think that you will be notifying people about the job?" The latter is a legitimate question that indicates to the search committee that you are seriously interested in the position. Another legitimate question would be, "Have you received all my supporting materials? Is there anything else that you need?" Again, this indicates your interest in the position without putting the employer on the spot.

You also may get phone calls before being asked for an interview. In the author's experience at Indiana University, the search committee had narrowed down the candidates to the top five. However, they could only afford to bring two people to campus for interviews. The search committee chairperson called and asked that additional materials be sent, which included copies of articles or papers and a letter stating research interests and priorities. At that time, a deadline was given for the search committee's decision, which at least gave the candidate a limit on time spent in reviewing writings. You only needed to be highly anxious for five days rather than an unknown amount of time.

Having survived the waiting time by the grace of God and good friends, you are finally rewarded with an interview.

THE INTERVIEW

The day has arrived, and you need to take a big deep breath. Tell yourself, "I know I'm good, and by the end of this day, they'll know I'm good too!" Then relax and be the person you are.

Interviews generally last a full day or more, so be prepared. Eat a big breakfast because you may not be able to eat the lovely lunch before you while you answer all the questions being thrown at you. Don't drink a lot of liquids because you may not have time to go to the bathroom for long periods of time. Dress appropriately and wear comfortable shoes as you may have a lot of walking to do. You might want to carry a leather envelope in which you have a portfolio containing your dissertation abstract or proposal, a class syllabus you have developed, proposals for presentations you have submitted, and a copy of a paper or article you have written. If these materials have already been submitted, you may still need the leather envelope for papers the search committee gives you.

You will meet many different people during the day. You will have an interview with the top administrator(s) in your department. You will meet with the head of your particular program or area, as well as with other faculty. You may meet with members of the search committee individually, as a group, or both. You may be asked to present an address on your research or other topic of interest to a group of faculty and students. There is no question that this will be a full day.

Throughout this day you will be asked questions. You may be asked to state your philosophy of your field as well as professional goals. You may also be asked what you would do with a particular program or class. Another area for questions will be your research interests and what you might do for grant proposals. Perhaps the most helpful thing you can do to prepare for these kinds of questions is to role play the interview with someone in your university who has been on a search committee. Two good friends of the author's spent three grueling hours in an interview-simulation situation asking the author the hardest questions that they could think of. This dress-rehearsal activity not only forces you to consolidate your thoughts, but it also gives you a sense of feeling at ease when the actual performance begins.

You also need to think about questions to ask the search committee. Don't hesitate to ask about salary and benefits. These are important considerations. You will want to know what the teaching load is as well as the advising load. Question the committee about tenure and criteria for tenure. You will also need to know about time and money available for research. Since service is an important part of a job, you should ask about restrictions on off-campus activities, such as consulting or in-service workshops. It is no secret that faculty salaries are notoriously low, so you may want to inquire about summer employment. You might also ask, especially the faculty, what they conceive the strengths of their program to be.

THE JOB HUNT / 125

In addition to job-related questions, there are personal questions that need to be answered. What kind of housing is available? If you have children, you will want to know about schools and additional programs for children. You may want to know something about the community in which the university is located. Are there cultural events? What about churches or religious organizations? What about medical personnel and hospitals? If you are a dater (or want to become one [see Chapter 8]) you may want to question whether it's a married couples town or if there are single men available. (This last question must be done subtly!)

The questions you ask and answer provide information to both you and the search committee about the "match" between you and that particular university. In a way, the situation is analogous to dating and marriage. The first interview is like that first date—a time to decide if you want to continue the relationship. (To continue the analogy, tenure becomes the marriage.)

Interviews, although threatening in one sense, can be a very positive experience. You are meeting with professionals in your field who also happen to be—in most instances—nice human beings. Remember that you also are a professional person and a nice human being.

DID YOU GET THE JOB?

Rarely are you asked to take a position on the day of the interview (the author, much to her delight, proved to be an exception). The search committee may have other candidates to interview, or the committee's choice may have to clear the Affirmative Action Office. You may have to wait for two or more weeks before hearing from the search committee. The waiting, again, can be a time of stress. In addition, another problem can occur that necessitates a major decision on your part. You may have been interviewed for more than one position, and the position you like least is offered to you before you have heard about the position you liked most. You may have to decide about the offer immediately. Don't accept the sure thing if you feel you will not be happy. It's risky, but if you're good you will get other offers. When this situation arises it is appropriate to call the search committee chairperson for the position you really want and ask for a time guideline for the committee's decision.

At the end of this long, time-consuming, anxiety-ridden experience, you will have been offered and will have accepted a position. With dissertation finished and a firm job commitment in hand, you are ready to begin the new life of the professional woman.

A POSTSCRIPT

Sue Vartuli asked me to add a postscript about the time between accepting the job and moving to your new life. We discovered that after the elation that accompanied the successful job search subsides, a new kind of anxiety emerges. We began to share with each other the fears of really being able to do a good job once we got where we wanted to be. We voiced the concern about tenure and began to realize that the years of struggling to stay in and complete the doctoral program were to be repeated in the struggle to gain tenure. We cried about having to leave the good friends who had become a part of our support system and questioned our abilities to make the move as persons as well as professionals. I shared with Sue my concerns about having to make the move as a single parent with two children, as well as the pain of having to decide to leave an older child in Ohio to finish high school.

In trying to capture the essence of the job-search experience, one might say that there was an ebb and flow of activity and inactivity, with periods of inactivity being marked by higher degrees of stress and anxiety. The final period of inactivity—between accepting the position and beginning the job—was a bittersweet time. There is no easy resolution to the concerns that emerge, but we feel that the strength that got us through the doctoral program will help us in this new period of our lives.

12

IS THE PH.D. EXPERIENCE
WORTH IT?: A DISCUSSION

After completing any serious long-term endeavor, there
comes a time to reflect on the experience. The following dialogue
is a transcript of a discussion the authors had prior to publication
of this book. We discussed two main questions: Is the Ph.D. experience worth it, personally and professionally? How have we
changed during the Ph.D. process? Both of these questions were
asked frequently during the graduate program. The following dialogue will reflect the struggles these 11 women faced as they came
to terms with the nature of higher education.

Sharon Barnett: I've been giving a lot of thought to the value of a
Ph.D. I have to keep forcing myself because I know that questioning the Ph.D. process is normal between the second and the third
year of the Ph.D. program. After two years I have lost sight of my
whole plan—my reasons for entering. As I compare notes with
other people, however, I find that the experience is not unusual.
The question of whether one should finish or not at this point is a
prevalent one. If I weren't so goal oriented I wouldn't be in the program. This is true for most of us. As I watch other people involved in the job search, taking new jobs, I find myself computing
the costs that are involved in obtaining a doctorate degree and I ask,
is it worth it?

At this time, I could give you more reasons why it is not worth
it than why it is. First of all, because I have come from a well-paid
position in college administration, it will take years to make up the
financial deficit. Secondly, I have had to move far from home and
leave two sons of high school and college age in another state. Initially, I decided that this was all right because it was justified by

the Ph.D. I don't think I could do that again. It is not worth it to be that far away from my kids. Also, not because of the Ph.D. process but because of other problems that the Ph.D. process aggravated, my 13-year-old daughter is now living with her father. So in no way would that be worth it again. I just can't think of enough reasons for going into a program, but what I'm trying to do at this time is look at the process as connected to a future, five, ten, fifteen years from now. I'm 43 at this time and I really believe, I need to believe and have faith, that out there the doctorate is going to in some way make some openings for me that couldn't be made otherwise.

My husband has been very interested in going to South America with the Peace Corps. Going there and giving up our material possessions appeals to both of us. I am bilingual; I would like to go to Mexico. I would like to be in a different culture, and I think that for both of us my Ph.D. may be one of the keys that will open doors that otherwise would be closed. Then it would be worth the process a million times over. But all things considered, the cost is too high for a wife and mother.

Linda Levstik: The experience for me has been very different, but I haven't had to leave a family as has Sharon. As far as whether the doctoral experience as a whole has been worth it—it has been a really good thing for me, in a lot of ways. It has convinced me of things about myself that I wasn't sure about: that I could handle things I hadn't seen myself doing before, that I could deal with situations I hadn't thought I'd be able to. For instance, the first year in grad school I was asked to introduce Lawrence Kohlberg. First of all, up until that year I hadn't known who he was. Then I found out that he was THE speaker for this conference, and here I was, this first-year TA, introducing him in front of all these people who already had their Ph.D.s. It scared me to death, but I stood up and found that I could do it. I could get up there and my voice didn't crack and I didn't pass out cold. Then I was asked to give a speech to a small group, and 200 people showed up. After that I figured I could handle public speaking.

Phyllis Saltzman Levy: I have a completely different perspective from Sharon and Linda because I have no children. I gave up nothing, to start with. This is something that my whole life literally has been focused toward so I've prepared for it. Is it worth it? Absolutely! Regardless of what I learned and the highs and the friendships, getting a Ph.D. meant that I finished an agenda and I'm free now to do all kinds of things. The world of research is open to me. I'm having such a wonderful time now that I am certified, initiated. It means all kinds of things, and I am finding lots of opportunities opening up because I am a doctor.

<u>Rosalind Williams</u>: What kinds of opportunities?

<u>Phyllis</u>: Being asked to speak, getting all kinds of goodies from the school system I work in, like being sent to conferences and getting days off. It just feels really good the whole way around. Both the product and the process were absolutely fabulous. I learned what it meant to feel terror. I had never felt terror before. [laughter] That's important, especially since I'm a teacher. Nothing had ever been hard for me before, but the qualifying exams were one of the hardest things I ever encountered in my life. And I made it! During the dissertation, I learned how to use my brain. I had this precious, no, ecstatic experience with Ross Mooney. I don't know if any of you know him. I was working with him 20-25 hours a week in direct contact. What that did for my mind you can't imagine. He taught me how to think. What a privilege that is! With a person that special! Writing the dissertation was the greatest thing I ever did in my life, all the way through. I just flew through that experience. It was just a really good thing. There have also been significant changes for me as a person such as those expressed in the chapter that I wrote for this book. I had no idea that any of the white male game was going on before my doctoral program. Not even an inkling. That realization did not even start until a whole year of my doctoral studies was completed.

<u>Sharon</u>: Phyllis, how old are you?

<u>Phyllis</u>: 29. I graduated when I was just barely 28. I started when I was 26. I had a master's already. That's my story.

<u>Rosemary Bolig</u>: My feelings are similar to most expressed, particularly Phyllis's sense of being freed. The Ph.D. process was worth it because it completes a pattern of my life that makes sense to me, though I initially did not make a conscious decision regarding what that pattern was to be. It was a self-actualizing experience. I was able to risk, to suspend others' judgments and society's expectations, and to concentrate my efforts at a level and in a manner theretofore perceived impossible. As to the future, I am still thinking and feeling about what the next pattern is to be. But this time <u>I</u> will make the choices!

<u>Bernice Smith</u>: I think I can say that it was worth it. When I began this program in 1976, I was a prekindergarten teacher for the Columbus public school system. I enjoyed teaching, and it was very hard giving up that salary. I believe then, as I do now, that one has to make sacrifices for something one really wants. I wanted to teach on the college level, and I knew I would have to get a Ph.D. degree; so I was willing to make any sacrifices necessary to obtain

this degree. I knew that getting this degree would put a great strain on my family, emotionally and financially. I convinced myself, with the help of my husband, that it would all be worth it in the end. I also rationalized that since my husband, Ervin, had gone through the experience of getting a Ph.D., I would benefit from knowing what it was like for him.

The fact that my husband would be on sabbatical the year I began my program and could give constant help and support to our son, Brian, who was two years old at the time, also helped me to make the decision to begin the program when I did. Family support means a lot, and we have always believed in this. In fact, when Ervin completed his program I typed his dissertation, and when I completed my program, he typed my dissertation. [cheers, clapping]

Yes, getting this degree has meant a great deal to me. When I graduated from high school, my mother said to me that I probably would not be able to go to college because we didn't have the money. I was the first in my family to become a college graduate. I have six siblings and only one, my brother, has graduated from college. He has a degree in engineering. I am the first and only one in my family with a Ph.D. degree, and although there were many, many hard times, I feel it was all worth it!

Linda: You do sacrifice a lot and you have to be willing to live with the person that you are when it is over. If you knew who you were going to be when you got out, you might change your mind about it.

Bernice: I value and treasure many of the experiences that I had. For example, I met J. McVicker Hunt when he was here in 1977 to speak at one of our conferences on campus. I had read about Hunt, but I never dreamed of meeting him. The evening following his keynote address, the chairman of our department invited a few graduate students to meet with Hunt informally at Schmidt's in German Village. This was quite an experience. He serenaded us. Can you imagine being serenaded by J. McVicker Hunt? He also talked with us at length about his research and experiences in the field of early childhood education.

Also, at the same conference that Linda spoke about, I introduced Kevin Ryan. He was also one of the keynote speakers. This was another great experience.

Linda: We were both in our first year.

Bernice: Right. First-year students.

Linda: And that first luncheon! We were so nervous, looking around at all those people, absolutely convinced that they were so much more intelligent.

Phyllis: I don't know what you're talking about.

Linda: Oh, in the department they have an introductory luncheon for T.A.s in September. They have it over at the faculty club. I remember listening to these people who had written books and done wonderful things and administered programs, and so on and I thought, oh, am I out of my league!

Rosalind: I've gone both ways in answering this question, but I think that basically this was a very worthwhile thing for me to have done. I see the experience as part of my mature phase of development, and I wouldn't be who I am today if I hadn't undergone it. I'm pretty pleased with myself, so it must have been O.K. to have done it. I was not one of those people who had very specific goals that I was going to meet in getting a doctorate. In fact, I sort of slid into it in a sense because I was in an education specialist program that somehow didn't get off the ground. They invited me to apply for the doctoral program, and I did. It was a very backdoor way of proceeding, but it is the way I tend to do a lot of things. I too had the experience of being a master of ceremonies for a conference that included doctoral students. Like some of you said, this kind of experience really gives one a sense of personal validity. One of my best experiences was a conference in which Jack Birch, who is kind of a grand old man in special education, was one of the speakers. He said he knew this conference was organized by graduate students; it never would have come off so well otherwise. We all just went— Yeah! The chapter for this book I wrote came right out of my insides. There were things that I dealt with there that weren't always good. I had some real tough times in school but here I am, surviving, doing well.

Mary Cay Wells: Unequivocally, for me it was worth it. It has been a personal challenge. I, too, lost income that I probably won't ever regain, but that is not the main issue. The whole experience is analogous to the Wizard of Oz for me. I guess I'm Dorothy!

Mary Ann McConnell: Who is the Wizard?

Mary Cay: The Wizard? Perhaps the university. But, like Dorothy, I already had in my own backyard or within myself the skills and knowledge that I needed to do what I wanted to do. When I began, I didn't have that insight, nor did I have the confidence to implement it. The whole experience gave me some more tools, it gave me theory, but basically it helped me appreciate what I already had within myself. It gave me what Dan Lortie calls a "subjective warrant," that is, permission to be myself. Some years ago a couple of mentors of mine said, "You'll end up in college teaching." I said,

"Oh, no, I'm not that smart." Yet here I am. I'm not any smarter than I was, but I'm teaching at the college level and loving it. Because I saw myself as "just a classroom teacher" I didn't believe that I could do what I'm doing now. Somehow these three years helped me see myself in another way.

Maybe I act a little bit differently to others now, and maybe I don't, but I feel that I've earned a credibility in the minds of some other people. I see it reflected in the way they regard me.

Mary Ann: I haven't finished my doctoral work yet. But, so far, the Ph.D. process has been worth it. I've enjoyed the intellectual stimulation that I've gotten from peers and classes and from profs in classes. I found the generals an interesting experience. The oral exams we don't talk about. Linda helped me survive that. After I came out of the orals I called her on the phone and I think we talked for 45 minutes. But at this point it has been worth it, and I'm really looking forward to writing the dissertation. One of the biggest challenges that I've found is fighting to maintain myself as the person I see myself being, as I want to be, and as I intend to stay. I have encountered some real conflicts with professors because of my determination to maintain my chosen identity. But at this point, yes, it has been worth it. I've enjoyed the whole environment. Ask me again after the dissertation is finished.

Sue Vartuli: Being in a new position, just starting a new career, I can say, yes, it is definitely worth it. I now have the abilities, knowledge, and, most importantly, the confidence to develop a teacher-training program. The best part of having a Ph.D. degree is that people respect what I say. I have some clout now. The knowledge is there, and the common sense has always been there, but now people listen to my ideas. It's a wonderful feeling. I have regained some of the feelings of self-worth that the doctoral experience had diminished.

Marion McNairy: "Is it worth it?" is not the question that I am confronted with now. The question now is "In what way will getting the Ph.D. impact on me as a whole person?" I'm more interested in the ways in which the Ph.D. will impact on me as a whole person. I can't respond to that question right now.

Phyllis: Anybody else? Is it worth it?

Linda: I think that for women who have been raised in an environment where you weren't supposed to be too smart and where you had to hide your brains, a Ph.D. program is one of the most exciting things that you can do. Suddenly there are all these women who enjoy being intelligent. You can have an intellectual relationship with another female and nobody thinks it's strange. It's wonderful! In that way, the Ph.D. was a blessing.

Sharon: Working for the doctorate is such an intense process that I wonder if you feel that you are the same person you were when you entered? Did your goals change? Did your concept of self change? What does such an intense process do in such a short period of time?

Phyllis: I can tell a story. But this might be a function of age too. That's a real problem for me. I think going from adolescence to adulthood in the same period as getting a Ph.D., you know, it is hard to separate out time. Anyway, there is a male that I worked for before the Ph.D. experience, and working for him was just like having my head in a vise. He squeezed. That was the feeling I experienced the whole time I worked for him. Finally, because of support from the central administration, I was able to get out of there and get into a place where I could think and talk and be a human being. I can't remember exactly how I functioned under his supervision, but I must have allowed myself to feel inferior even though this man was not someone that I respected at that time. After I got my degree, the man came to see me about something, and he came into my classroom. I was the teacher and he was an administrator, remember. He came in and sat down next to me at the round table, and he literally shook as he talked to me. And you know, it was suddenly an entirely different situation. Our former positions were reversed. I was completely at ease, and he wasn't. I hadn't even opened my mouth and he was afraid of me, simply because I had a Ph.D. It is just a whole new ballgame now. We spent a lot of time getting rid of his nervousness, which he never bothered to do for me. It's like being another person in many, many respects.

Linda: It makes a difference in the responses that other people make to you. I think there is a definite difference when people find out that you are a Ph.D. They respond very differently to me as Doctor _____ than they did to me as Mrs. _____. But that's something that other people impose on you, not a change in your own self.

Sharon: The idea that Mary Cay shared—subjective want—really intrigued me, and I think a large part of my coming into the Ph.D. program had to do with a long-term subjective want, one related to my way of seeing myself. It started with the desire to obtain a medical degree. When I started I was a premed student back in the late fifties. To be a human being I had to have a doctorate. So I wonder if maybe I'm not verifying who I am by satisfying my subjective want.

Linda: In what specific ways have you seen yourself changing?

Sharon: I experienced a real loss of self-concept. I've always perceived myself as an extremely strong person, and that also went along with the positions I had. Then at 40, coming back into the subjective role of student, I developed a chip on my shoulder. As a doctoral student I was working for people who were administering programs that were a lot smaller than the ones I had had to deal with when I was an administrator, and here they were having me go around with a piece of paper and a pencil taking little notes behind them. It hit me as being humorous. I thought, what the hell am I doing here? Accepting the role of student required quite an adjustment for me. So I felt a loss of self-concept.

Linda: Sharon, do you think that your age added to the problem of adjustment?

Sharon: Yes, I think age had something to do with it. That's why I asked Phyllis her age. She probably is going through a major developmental transition, and I think in the early forties there is another transition going on. The validation I'm looking for I think I've already found, and now maybe I don't need the Ph.D. I can accept that I have these skills and these abilities and these interests, and the Ph.D. doesn't necessarily put a stamp of approval on me.

Linda: I think that before I always looked like I had a lot of self-confidence. At least people have always told me that I had a confident bearing. Now it is real. My goals have changed radically. I came in thinking, O.K., my husband is established here; he's got a good position. He loves what he is doing, but I am no longer satisfied with what I am doing. The program bought me time, time to decide what I wanted to do next. I had some ideas about that and then, when I was almost finished with the degree, I realized that I didn't want to do any of those things—that I had some pretty strong ideas about new things I wanted to try, and they didn't necessarily involve staying around here. I think that is one of the reasons I didn't start looking for a job for a long time. I was afraid that it was going to be an enormous crisis when it finally came. Now I feel more in control of things and more willing to take risks.

Mary Cay: I'm the same person, but I think as you do, Linda, that my self-confidence has increased. Of course, with that increase came the ability to use what I have, and I can do more. I haven't sorted out fully all that it means to me. There are some deep meanings, hard for me to know clearly, let alone say. Part of it has to do with staving off old age. I have filled myself to the point where I can have a much richer old age, having met interesting people, having read good books, and having had the opportunity to think the things I did. I'm terribly grateful that I'm not going to be patroniz-ingly relegated to senior citizen status! The Ph.D. experience blurred age lines, too. It's a good feeling not to be bound by one's own, or anyone else's, chronological age.

Rosalind: I would like to say something about one of the things Sharon was talking about before: not only what did you come out like but what did the Ph.D. process do to you? Both physiological-ly and psychologically it did a lot to me. I increased the amount of stress that I put myself under tremendously by going in. That may not be true for everybody, but for me it certainly was. The jobs that I did before were not nearly as stressful as going to graduate school. What I did was set myself up for a lifetime of stress. I may or may not go back to a job that is less stressful for me, but if I do, I will not be completely satisfied and I'll really have to change my expectations. Because of the people that I have inter-acted with and the kinds of things that I have seen, I now have a lot of pressures that I put on myself that I never would have put on be-fore. And sometimes it is still very hard for me to sort out what I want to take on and what I don't. I say to myself every day, "You should be doing this, and you should be doing that." I feel guilty if I relax.

Phyllis: Can you relax?

Rosalind: Oh yeah, sure I do. I'm not a real workaholic kind of person. I never have been. But I have learned to take care of my-self better. The thing that I wrote in my little vignette about finally realizing that I'm the one for the job of taking care of myself is of real significance to me. Now I'm in the process of learning how to do that better. But I wouldn't have come so far in this regard if I hadn't experienced the stress levels that I did in graduate school.

Rosemary: I've changed. I value myself more and am more self-confident. I am also more aware of the need to develop a balance in my life. As a single person, although friends have been very significant, I feel as if the past three years, perhaps out of neces-sity, I've put a disproportionate amount of effort and time into my academic and professional life. I am now beginning to regain a broader perspective. Some behaviors related to professional ex-pectations have changed as well. I spend less time on minutiae, am more task oriented, and can have several projects in process simultaneously. I look forward to continued change, and feel that the Ph.D. experience was an accelerator. New challenges and new risks will evolve or be sought out. Yet I will undertake them with a very different attitude than before I completed the Ph.D.

__Bernice__: I think I'm a much stronger person because of the experience. I feel now that I can do almost anything. I've always thought of myself as a strong person, but after getting into the program, I wondered if I was as strong as I thought I was. I think people expect you to act differently after you get the degree. In fact, a friend of mine congratulated me after I graduated, and then he went and told my husband, "Oh, Bernice is the same, she didn't act any different." And I hear that a lot. I hope that I am the same in the sense of caring and being sensitive to people. I don't ever want to be bigheaded, excuse the expression, but I want to feel good about what I know and willing to share what knowledge I have. I feel good about myself.

__Mary Ann__: You commented about being sensitive to people. This is the problem that I've had the most difficulty dealing with as I have been going through the program. I'm a person who is very interested in people, and I'm the kind of nut who will sit down in shopping centers and airports and watch people go by. They totally fascinate me. When I am working with or developing some kind of a friendship with university people, I not only want to know what they think intellectually, but I want to know who they are outside the academic setting. I find that many people in the university setting are not open to this kind of relationship. I find that some professors are very threatened by it. I think that is one of the reasons that I have difficulty with professors. As a child I was brought up with the idea that you don't kowtow to anyone. You are as good as everybody else. And so I don't often worship at the shrine. That causes problems, and so does the fact that I'm so very open with people. Personally, this is very difficult for me to deal with because I like to know what makes people tick. I like to know what they think. I'm having to revamp my ways of relating to people in an academic setting simply because it turns people off. I find having to do this very disturbing, because I want to know about these people and I want to know where they are coming from and where they are going. What I have found most personally disturbing is not being able to develop the kind of friendships with professors and other graduate students that I have developed with you, the kind in which I can sit down and talk with someone on a very personal level. Without this group, I probably would have dropped out of the program because it was just so much in conflict with who I am. I don't think I could have survived.

__Linda__: Kind of learning the rules of the game?

__Mary Ann__: Right. This is one of the things that I sometimes think about in terms of a job. Once I finish, what kind of setting do I want to go into? One of my goals has never been to teach at "the top 10."

I couldn't care less. I want to go into a teachers' college. I want to teach people who want to become teachers, and I am looking forward to that—really taking a look at the people who are involved in that situation, working with them on a daily basis. I want personable people who want friendships over and above the academic setting, and that's one of my goals—a university that has human beings as professors.

Phyllis: Since the doctoral experience I'm much more conscious of how I do things. That's a huge change for me. I used to do things unreflectively and now I can look at myself in a different way. The other big change is that I'm able to produce far more than I ever could before. That's a direct result of having observed one professor's work through his whole career and seeing how he worked and learned to be a producer. I never would have thought of myself as a writer, and this morning when I was taking my walk it occurred to me, all I do all day long is write. So I guess maybe I _am_ a writer. Those are the two big changes.

Sue: I feel I have changed personally. I now value "authentic" people more. I don't like shallow game players, and I'm getting wiser to the type of people in the world. I am becoming somewhat more cynical or perhaps growing up and not being so idealistic about others. I have always thought people are basically good and caring. This experience has taught me that there are quite a few egocentric prima donnas in this world. We need all kinds of people to make the world go round, but I will stay away from the steamrollers. I have learned some valuable lessons.

Katherine Tracey: I have just finished reading the transcript of the group discussion about the personal and professional results of being part of a Ph.D. program. I only wish that 1,100 miles had not separated me from participating firsthand in that conversation. I found myself saying, "Oh yes, me too!!" or "Oh, it was different for me!" so many times.

For me the most important elements of those three-and-a-half years were the people and the process. The network of women I described in my chapter, other fellow graduate students, and professors challenged me to stretch and grow. In the process I discovered some of my own untapped resources. I gained new respect for my own creativity and an understanding of my own fallibility.

For me, juggling roles (I have a young daughter) was the greatest challenge of being female. Keeping things at home running smoothly and having the time and energy to enjoy Rebecca did not always fit with the demands of graduate school. The continual balancing act caused me to stretch and also triggered the rethinking of some of the responsibilities I had assumed without questioning. I had unwittingly accepted the "superwoman" image: the notion that I could and should be able to do everything for everyone with the greatest of ease. That is a dangerous pitfall, an inflated view of self and an impossible task.

Several of you mentioned significant people. My dissertation committee chairperson, John B. Hough, was such a person for me. He has a rare gift of caring about and challenging the whole person. I thrived under his guidance because I felt both his support and his challenge. In that environment I feel I tapped resources I didn't know existed.

I would choose to do it all again. Easy—NO! Painful—YES! Results—UNCERTAIN?! My life has been changed in many ways by the people and the experience. I view life as an unfolding process and the Ph.D. experience will continue to influence how I unfold the next scenes.

Sue: We all have had poignant experiences to share. These episodes in our lives say a lot about our culture, society, educational system, and the times in which we live. By sharing parts of our lives in a group, we have had an opportunity to reflect introspectively, benefiting from the camaraderie and genuine caring of friends. We will cherish this rewarding experience in days to come. By writing and recording our experiences, we hope others will gain some insight into the socialization process of obtaining a Ph.D.

SUGGESTED READINGS

Astin, H. S. The Women Doctorate in America: Origins, Career, and Family. New York: Russell Sage Foundation, 1969.

Astin describes the results of a comprehensive study of women with doctoral degrees in America. The findings dispel many myths, e.g., that women do not utilize their training. Of all women who received their doctorates in 1958 and 1959, 91 percent were employed. Ten years after receiving their doctorates, over half of the women studied had achieved the status of full or associate professorship.

Dohrenwend, Barbara, and Bruce Dohrenwend (eds.). Stressful Life Events: Their Nature and Effects. New York: Wiley, 1974.

The Dohrenwends have edited an excellent overview of the ways that stress is induced by the socialization process. Varied perspectives from many authors are presented.

Foxley, C. G. Nonsexist Counseling: Helping Women and Men Redefine Their Roles. Dubuque, Iowa: Kendall/Hall, 1979.

Three major topics—stereotyping of sex roles, the significance for counselors of social change, and training for nonsexist counseling—are presented in order to assist counselors, educators, and others in the helping professions to become more alert to the deleterious effects of sex-role stereotyping on human potential. Implications for varying roles and new models for counseling are explored.

French, Marilyn. The Women's Room. New York: Jove, 1977.

French looks at the graduate school experience from a woman's point of view and demonstrates that the real support group within the academic setting is other students. She also provides a realistic view of the stresses and strains that women must endure in order to obtain a graduate degree.

Henley, Nancy M. Body Politics: Power, Sex, and Nonverbal Communication. Englewood Cliffs, N.J.: Prentice-Hall, 1977.

We live in a context of power that is unevenly distributed. Non-verbal behaviors that express dominance and subordination between nonequals parallel those behaviors used by males and females, respectively. Henley has pioneered in the areas of nonverbal communication and power, analyzing them from a feminist viewpoint.

Hennig, Margaret, and Anne Jardim. The Managerial Woman. New York: Simon and Schuster, 1977.

A must for the career-oriented female and sensitive male, it provides a road map to the understanding of the people who run organizations and the differences between how females and males think.

Katz, Joseph, and Rodney Hartnett (eds.). Scholars in the Making: The Development of Graduate and Professional Students. Cambridge, Mass.: Ballinger, 1976.

This book offers a refreshing look at the student in higher education. It is a comprehensive, factual book that provides insight into the problems facing graduate students.

L'Engle, Madeline. A Circle of Quiet. New York: Seabury Press, 1979.

Primarily using materials from her journals, L'Engle shares personal experiences in nurturing creativity. She provides a valuable role model as a woman who has combined a productive writing career with strong family commitments. Her book shares some of the joys and struggles in that ongoing process.

Molloy, John T. The Woman's Dress for Success Book. New York: Warner Books, 1977.

Molloy did extensive research to discover clothing that would give women credibility. Based on these data, he makes specific recommendations to women about how to manipulate clothing choices to draw favorable responses from those they meet.

Rossi, A. S., and A. Caldewood (eds.). Academic Women on the Move. New York: Russell Sage Foundation, 1973.

A collection of papers analyzing the history and social status of women in academe. Studies on academic women's recruitment, careers, and productivity are presented in order to sensitize persons to the hazards of sex discrimination and to encourage further investigation of this all-too-pervasive social injustice.

SURVEY FORM

Date _____

Survey Form

The following form is a survey to collect information on your graduate experiences. The information we are collecting will be used
to survey readers on their educational experiences and readers'
reactions to the book. The descriptive data we collect may be the
source for a future research study or perhaps a revision of this book.

1. Age _____ City _____ State _____

2. Female _____

   Male _____

3. Education level (Check highest degree obtained and write in the
   year you graduated.)

   Degree   Year

   HS _____   _____

   BS _____   _____

   MS _____   _____

   PhD ____   _____

   EdD ____   _____

   MD ____   _____

   Other ____   _____ (please specify) _____

4. Are you currently enrolled in a graduate program? yes _____
   no _____ What degree? _____

5. Present occupation _____

6. Which chapter in this book was most helpful and why?

141

7. In preparing for general exams, did you find it most helpful to:
   a. study intensively a few weeks before
   b. study for specific questions delineated by your committee members
   c. review notes and research papers used in course work
   d. submit possible questions to committee members that you wished to write on because they were of interest to you

8. How would you generally describe the qualifying exam experience?
   a. extremely helpful
   b. very stressful
   c. an ordeal to be survived
   d. a waste of time

9. What more than anything else helped you through the dissertation experience?
   a. support of family and friends
   b. a very supportive and knowledgeable committee
   c. a well-defined and well-organized research project
   d. my own determination
   e. a combination of all of these
   f. others

10. Are there additional facets of surviving in a predominantly white male institution that were not included in the chapter, "Surviving in a Predominantly White Male Institution"? Please be specific in your descriptions.

11. As the general or comprehensive exam seems to present the most stress for the Ph.D. student, what alternatives would you suggest to this process or what alternatives are you aware of?

12. As a person in a graduate program, were you aware of any recurring or chronic illnesses affecting a number of students in the program?

13. Were there specific times in the doctoral process you sought support from your fellow students? yes _____ no _____

14. Describe these specific times briefly.

15. Did you experience disruption of an intimate relationship immediately before, during, or after doctoral study? yes____ no____

16. Can you describe the timing and reasons for the breakup briefly?

17. Are you married? yes ____ no ____

18. Do you have children? yes ____ no ____

19. Do you have a career? yes ____ no ____

20. What are some of the adjustments you have faced in balancing family needs with a career? Please be specific.

21. At what ages did you begin and complete your Ph. D. program?

22. How did/do your experiences as a mature student parallel or diverge from those recounted in "Grandma! What Big Plans You've Got!"?

23. Did your educational experiences prepare you for the actual available jobs?
    yes ____ no ____ More than one type of job? yes ____ no ____

24. Which source of information was the most helpful to you throughout your job search?

    ____ 1. your adviser

    ____ 2. department chairperson

    ____ 3. other faculty members

    ____ 4. students

    ____ 5. Chronicle of Higher Education

    ____ 6. professional journals

    ____ 7. university personnel placement office

    ____ 8. other (please specify)

25. Are you:

_____ first born

_____ second born

_____ third born

_____ fourth or later born

ABOUT THE EDITOR AND THE CONTRIBUTORS

SHARON BARNETT is an assistant professor teaching early childhood education courses at Memphis State University. Until entering the Ph.D. program in 1978, she served as director of continuing education at California Lutheran College. She was a faculty/ field supervisor in human services at Western Washington University following an administrative appointment in supplementary training/continuing education at California State University—Chico.

Dr. Barnett has served in Head Start programs over the past 12 years as a teacher, consultant, and child development associate college instructor. She holds a B.A. from California State University—Chico in psychology and an M.A. from the same institution in education administration. Her Ph.D. from The Ohio State University in early and middle childhood education was completed in 1981.

ROSEMARY A. BOLIG is an assistant professor of family relations and human development at The Ohio State University. Previous to 1973 she was involved in educational and play programs for hospitalized children and their families.

Dr. Bolig has published and presented papers in the area of child development, and particularly on hospitalized children. Her publications have appeared in the Journal of the Association for the Care of Children's Health.

Dr. Bolig holds a B.S. and an M.Ed. from Pennsylvania State University, University Park, Pennsylvania, and a Ph.D. from The Ohio State University.

LINDA S. LEVSTIK is an assistant professor at the University of Kentucky.

Dr. Levstik has published in the areas of children's literature and social studies. Her articles and reviews have appeared in Reading Ladders to Human Relations, Theory Into Practice, Checklist, and the OCSS Review.

Dr. Levstik holds a B.S. in Education from Capital University and an M.A. and Ph.D. from The Ohio State University.

PHYLLIS SALTZMAN LEVY is an educational writer and consultant. She has held a variety of teaching positions, including grades two through eight, and university instruction.

Dr. Levy has published in the area of education. Her articles have appeared in Middle School Journal, Teaching Exceptional Children, National Association of Secondary School Principals Bulletin, and the Professional Educator.

Dr. Levy holds a B.S., M.S., and Ph.D. from The Ohio State University.

MARY ANN McCONNELL is a lecturer, department of education, Xavier University, Cincinnati. She plans to finish her Ph.D. in the autumn quarter of 1981 at The Ohio State University.

Ms. McConnell holds a B.S.Ed. and an M.S.Ed. in elementary education from Ohio University in Athens. She has been an elementary school teacher, remedial reading teacher, field consultant, and editor for an educational publisher.

MARION R. McNAIRY is assistant professor of early childhood education at Indiana University, Bloomington, where she also serves as director of the university nursery school.

Dr. McNairy has been a program consultant for nursery schools and day-care centers both in this country and in the Virgin Islands.

Dr. McNairy holds a B.A. from San Francisco State University, an M.S. from Ohio University, and a Ph.D. from The Ohio State University.

BERNICE D. SMITH is assistant professor of education at The Ohio State University—Marion. She has been a prekindergarten teacher for the Columbus public school system and the director of the Evanston Neighbors At Work Head Start Program in Illinois.

Dr. Smith has served as a consultant for Head Start and has given numerous workshops, presentations, and lectures on "Parent Involvement" and "Early Childhood Education."

Dr. Smith holds a B.A. from Paine College, Augusta, Georgia, an M.Ed. from Erikson Institute for Early Education, Loyola University, Chicago, and a Ph.D. from The Ohio State University.

KATHERINE O. TRACEY is developing and directing a comprehensive school volunteer program for the school system of Sarasota County, Florida. Before moving back home to Sarasota in 1978, she taught German, worked as a middle school curriculum coordinator, and advised undergraduate students at The Ohio State University.

Dr. Tracey has written and consulted on using a problem-solving process to improve human interaction. Her doctoral research involved studying proxemics (nonverbal dimension of space and distance), and then helping teachers apply this information to use classroom space more effectively.

Dr. Tracey holds a B.A. from the College of Wooster in Ohio, and an M.A. and Ph.D. from The Ohio State University.

SUE A. VARTULI is an assistant professor of early childhood education at the University of Missouri—Kansas City, Kansas City, Missouri. She has developed the early childhood undergraduate program and is currently designing the graduate program in early childhood education. Dr. Vartuli was involved in establishing and administering The Ohio State University Child Care Program before she returned to graduate school.

Dr. Vartuli has published in the area of early childhood education. Her articles have appeared in Childhood Education and Education Digest. Dr. Vartuli holds a B.S. from State University College of New York at Oneonta and a Ph.D. from The Ohio State University.

MARY CAY WELLS is assistant professor of education at Otterbein College, Westerville, Ohio. She has been an elementary classroom teacher and staff developer, and currently does consulting in teacher selection.

Dr. Wells has published in the area of curriculum. Her articles have appeared in T.I.P., Education Forum, and The Professional Educator.

Dr. Wells holds a B.A. from Otterbein College, an M.A. from Bowling Green State University in Ohio, and a Ph.D. from The Ohio State University.

ROSALIND WILLIAMS is currently the coordinator of early education at Nisonger Center, The Ohio State University. Dr. Williams is an adjunct assistant professor in the departments of early and middle childhood education and family relations and human development at OSU. She has been on the faculty at OSU in the department of early and middle childhood education and an assistant professor at the University of Cincinnati.

She received her Ed.D. in early childhood special education from the University of Cincinnati.